MW00679341

AND God SAID "Go!"

Following God in a Culture of Chaos

AND GOD SAID "GO!"

Following God In a Culture of Chaos

LEROY LAWSON

Standard
PUBLISHING
CINCINNATI, OHIO

ISBN 0-7847-7169-3

Edited by Lynn Perrigo
Cover design by Liz Howe Design

Standard Publishing, Cincinnati, Ohio
A division of Standex International Corporation
© 2003 by Standard Publishing
Printed in the United States of America

Contents

1

More Than a Dreamer

Genesis 41:1-57

When I was a beggarly boy
    And lived in a cellar damp,
I had not a friend nor a toy,
    But I had Aladdin's lamp.
When I could not sleep for the cold,
    I had fire enough in my brain,
And builded with roofs of gold
    My beautiful castles in Spain.
                    —James Russell Lowell

Lowell's language is dated now, but Aladdin's lamp still fires young imaginations, especially those of boys and girls who have seen Disney's screen version of the old fantasy. What young person has not longed for a genie to make a special wish come true? Who hasn't wanted to escape the perils of here for the paradise of there? What young Joseph could have done with Aladdin's lamp! The poet's cellar-bound "beggarly boy" and Jacob's favorite son have a lot in common. Friendless, penniless, apparently futureless, they were treated like refuse on the human garbage dump. But even in that deprived—some would say depraved—condition, they had secret resources. They could dream. And they could believe.

In Joseph's case, the dreams came true. This is one dreamer who bears studying. But what we learn is that he is more than a dreamer. He is a dreamer who understands what he dreams.

A Discerning Visionary

Students in my "flower-children era" college classes predicted they would never forget the popular film, *The Graduate*. While I taught at Milligan College (1965 to 1973), no other movie in those turbulent, near-revolutionary days gripped young collegians like this one. In the film, young Benjamin (Dustin Hoffman) has a joyless, clandestine affair with the experienced seductress, Mrs. Robinson (Anne Bancroft). For weeks they sleep together, but when he tries to learn something about this woman with whose body he has had free reign, she turns reluctant and elusive. He can't pique her interest in anything. She's bored with life. As a student she had studied art, but when, already pregnant, she married Mr. Robinson, she gave up her studies and her curiosity about any art style. Once, perhaps, she had had a dream, but that was long ago and intellectually far away. When she entered into her boringly conventional marriage, she lost her dream and then found escape only in sexual affairs with unformed young men whose bodies she used but whose persons meant nothing to her.

No one is to be pitied more than the person without a dream.

Nothing is more commonplace than to desert one's dreams when bested by disappointment, defeat, fear, or mere routine. There are too many Mrs. Robinsons in this world.

Which is why we turn with fascination to the story of Joseph. With a strength we admire but have a hard time imitating, this man would not give up. His father coddled him; his older brothers despised and sold him into slavery, hoping never to see him again; and his master's wife slandered and had him tossed into prison. Yet in spite of everything, he could still dream.

More than just dream. He could comprehend his dreams. And he could interpret others' dreams. Thanks to this remarkable, God-given power, he could see the future. God had given him the makings of a leader.

When a political candidate asked John W. Gardner, an astute student of leadership, the most important thing that a leader could do for the American people "at this moment in history," he said, "Give them back their future."[1] There is never a moment when this is not the task of a leader. The baker and the cupbearer, languishing in prison with Joseph, turned to him not just to gain insight into their strange dreams, but to learn about the future. His brothers, infuriated by his claim that he would rule over them someday, were maddened by his vision of the future. They couldn't abide his arrogance. They would never bend their knees to their spoiled, bragging half brother. They didn't like it, but what Joseph had told them was indeed the truth. He had showed them the future.

England's Winston Churchill remarked early in his career that the most desirable qualification for a politician "is the ability to foretell what is going to happen tomorrow, next week, next month, and next year." Then he wryly added, "and to have the ability afterwards to explain why it didn't happen."[2] Churchill was a most astute politician, but he wasn't a Joseph. Jacob's son, obviously, wasn't your ordinary politician. Life would have been easier if he had been. His dreams got him into trouble. His God-given ability to give people a future led to slavery and imprisonment; it also propelled his rise to official power, which a cynic might note is still a type of slavery, but with more mobility.

I am calling Joseph a *discerning* visionary because when he interpreted Pharaoh's dreams to him, he didn't stop with a simple explanation. He slipped seamlessly from interpretation to unsolicited advice, which is always a dangerous move:

> And now let Pharaoh look for a discerning and wise
> man and put him in charge of the land of Egypt. Let
> Pharaoh appoint commissioners over the land to take a
> fifth of the harvest of Egypt during the seven years of
> abundance. They should collect all the food of these good
> years that are coming and store up the grain under the
> authority of Pharaoh, to be kept in the cities for food. This
> food should be held in reserve for the country, to be used
> during the seven years of famine that will come upon
> Egypt, so that the country may not be ruined by the
> famine (Genesis 41:33-36).

Genesis records that "the plan seemed good to Pharaoh and to all his officials" (41:37). It's a good thing. Joseph still hadn't learned tact. His abrupt assertiveness had prompted his brothers to dispose of him. A defensive Pharaoh could easily have done the same thing, but this king wasn't defensive, apparently. Fortunately for Joseph, rather than take offense at his prisoner's boldness, Pharaoh recognized his wisdom. This Hebrew was more than a dreamer. He could produce.

I'm impressed that the Egyptian court so quickly approved Joseph's plan, especially since it meant handing power over to a foreigner. This is the stuff of corporate warfare! A CEO's minions rarely welcome an outsider, especially one on a fast track to promotion. Sometimes, though, only the outsider can deliver a "future." The insiders are too enmeshed in the status quo, too highly invested in things as they've always been to effect the changes the future demands. The best thing a new leader brings into the organization is his freedom from the past and his vision of a new, more effective future. Thus Joseph.

A Wise Administrator

Not that it is easy for the new guy to bring about the future he sees. One of the inherent risks of leadership is in that gap between heightened expectations ("give them a future") and the reality that can be delivered. We see this every four years in America as our presidential candidates paint their promised paradise in Technicolor™ for their adoring audiences. We as voters listen to their promises, weigh their words, and cast our ballots for the one whose picture we like best. Then we wait. We know what's coming. Almost immediately, the gap between promise and delivery appears . . . and widens, and disillusionment sets in. Our new leader isn't going to keep his word. His campaign promises were just that—mere promises. Max DePree, one of America's outstanding CEOs a generation ago, believed that "keeping promises is what leadership is about." Period. If he was right, it's no wonder we feel so disappointed by our elected officials. They break promises.

Not that keeping promises is easy. John Gardner observed, "Leaders are almost never as much in charge as they are pictured to be, followers almost never as submissive as one might imagine."[3] Anyone who has to juggle the conflicting demands of democratic leadership will be tempted to envy Joseph's free administrative reign before and during the famine. Only in a crisis are leaders allowed such sway. Seldom can they accomplish so much. Secretary of State Colin L. Powell, reflecting on his years as a military officer, writes, "Leadership is the art of accomplishing more than the science of management says is possible."[4] Management deals with the situation as is; leadership changes the situation. Joseph was astute at both.

General Powell rightly distinguishes between the two. Today, decades after his death, leadership and management experts still argue over Franklin D. Roosevelt's presidential style. You may disagree with him politically or philosophically and even debate whether he was good or bad for the country, but you are forced to admit he was one of the most powerful leaders ever to occupy the White House. Volumes have been written on his eccentric administrative practices, but few deny his nation's debt of gratitude for leading America through the Great Depression and then—hard on its heels—World War II. Roosevelt probably scored higher as a leader than as a manager, but even as an administrator, he had an uncanny ability that explains his remarkable success. He intuitively knew how to select the right person for the right job, whether in the top echelon of administration or on the lower rungs, and then release him or her to do it.

Just one instance will have to stand for many. We know about this one because the man involved became one of America's top media entertainers. The navy had refused Arthur Godfrey a commission at the start of World War II because of some old hip and knee injuries. When Mrs. Roosevelt got the word, she pleaded his case with the president. He had earlier commanded the navy himself, so he didn't hesitate to call the responsible officer on Godfrey's behalf. He asked, "Can he walk?"

Told that he could, Mr. Roosevelt barked, "Give him a commission, then. I can't walk and I'm the commander-in-chief!"[5]

Godfrey served loyally and well. Roosevelt had intervened wisely. He refused to let the regulations of the bureaucracy overrule sound judgment. He led.

Joseph's subsequent career as administrator proved him to be both a leader and manager. He saved the nation from hunger. Today, I suppose we'd call Joseph the "grain czar," since the king handed him total authority for hoarding the grain during the fruitful years and doling it out when the famine struck. He was so successful, he was able to feed not only the Egyptians but also aliens like his family. Blessed is an organization that is led by someone who can dream a future— and successfully lead his followers into it.

A Loyal Subordinate

I probably would not have paid any attention to Joseph's loyalty to his superiors Potiphar and Pharaoh if I hadn't been an administrator for most of my life. Loyalty is a virtue both wonderful and rare. If you asked me to describe the ideal employee, I'd be tempted to put this quality at the head of the list: loyalty to the mission, to the leader, to one's peers, and certainly to one's subordinates. You know the old test of loyalty, don't you? Here it is: "If you were in charge, would I be safe?" That is, would you be as loyal to me (as a subordinate, fellow worker, or friend) as you would want me to be to you? It's a bigger issue than mere personal allegiance. It implies your faithfulness to your assigned mission (one that I, too, serve) and to God who is, after all, *your* superior.

I have often quoted Eugene V. Debs, who was the great early twentieth-century labor leader. He was frequently condemned for his socialist political views. You don't have to agree with his opinions, however, to admire his character. He was arrested in 1918 and convicted for violating the Espionage Act. Before receiving his sentence on September 14, 1918, he delivered to the court what his biographers consider his most eloquent speech. It has remained an inspiration for generations of leaders of all political stripes: "While there is a lower class, I am in it; while there is a criminal element, I am of it; and while there is a soul in prison, I am not free." That, in essence, is loyalty. No matter what they do to me, I will be true to you. (Debs was sentenced to ten years in prison for his convictions, but President Harding later commuted the sentence to three years.)

Over the past couple of decades, what was once seen as a virtue is now often considered a liability. Not so long ago, young people were advised to get a job with a good company and to be a loyal employee, and the company would take care of you. So General Motors, Ford Motor Company, General Electric, and other major corporations could count on their "company men." We don't hear much about this species anymore. Today's employment counselors advise men and women to think of themselves as independent contractors, to negotiate the best deals they can get, and not to hesitate to jump ship if their company isn't giving them what they want. No wonder. Companies no longer offer lifetime security for their employees; in a recession, they'll announce thousands of layoffs, some-

times without benefits. "So what good is loyalty?" the fired
employees ask.

As a result, the workplace has lost a sense of community
and mutual security. Contract negotiations pit management
against labor and supervisors against subordinates. Everyone is
out to get what is best for Number One. Unfortunately, on this
matter Christian organizations—churches and parachurch
agencies, colleges, and universities—are hard to distinguish
from their secular counterparts. What seems to be missing is a
sense of devotion to a cause and the mutual care that defines
community. How can I really give myself to a mission or to my
co-workers when "it's all about me"?

So the negotiation-weary administrator looks with longing
on Joseph's service to his king and his king's country. Later,
when he takes such good care of his family, that same sense of
loyalty asserts itself again. Joseph does not forsake his own.
He's like Jesus, who could report to His Father, "I have brought
you glory on earth by completing the work you gave me to do"
(John 17:4). He didn't forsake His Father even though His loyalty cost Him His life.

Some Christian writers focus on what Jesus did: His death
on the cross, His remarkable teaching, His amazing miracles,
His modeling of full humanity, and so on. Others zero in on
what He didn't do: write a book, found a college, foment a revolution, construct a religion. But the Gospel accounts stress primarily Jesus' faithfulness to the Father who sent Him and the
cause for which He came. He could be counted on. He was
loyal.

A Faithful Sufferer

The subject of loyalty doesn't usually come up except in
relation to its cost. Loyalty is admired because it perseveres *in
spite of*.

Jesus was true to His Father's will *in spite of* Satan's wiles and the allure of his temptations. Moses earned our admiration because he never deserted his post as Israel's savior *in spite of* his countrymen's nearly constant complaining. The apostle Paul succeeded in planting Christianity among the Gentiles *in spite of* persecution, trials, imprisonments, and heartaches.

And the hero of this story, Joseph, refused to retaliate against his brothers or depart from his God *in spite of* betrayal, dungeon, and incredible hardship. He was, like Jesus after him, in many ways "a man of sorrows and acquainted with grief." But also like Jesus, he held steady *in spite of* setbacks. Robertson Davies in *The Manticore* disparages "the luxury of easy despair." You can't help wondering whether Joseph ever afforded himself such a luxury. The Genesis account never offers so much as a hint of it. Because of his deep faith, did Joseph believe, as Paul later taught us, that God always works for the good of those who love Him (Romans 8:28)? Did he suspect God had something better in store for him? Could he have guessed that his deprivations were preparing him for the great demands that would be laid on him later? Don't you suspect he later often reviewed those early dreams he repeated to his brothers? They led to his downfall then, but they must have sustained him on many a lonely night when he had nothing else to comfort him.

Such "toughening up" seems an indispensable ingredient in a person's training for leadership, doesn't it? Think of Moses' years in exile, Jesus' wilderness temptations, David's years on the run from King Saul, John the Baptist's spartan diet of locusts and wild honey. Even now, when we are seeking someone to lead our country, don't we still respond to tales of wartime valor or log cabin poverty? We want to know our leaders can take whatever life throws at them—and still remain faithful! No Benedict Arnolds need apply, please.

Think of all the people you know, famous and unknown, who "have it made." Wealth, education, the glittery trappings of culture—they have it all. Author John Cheever says the main emotion of such people is not elation but disappointment. I would add that often the main characteristic of such people is moral weakness. Success has softened them. Perhaps this is why Joseph had to suffer—to test his mettle, surely, but to toughen his resolve as well.

Some time ago I read Thomas Mallon's *A Book of One's Own*, an interesting study of personal diaries. In his introduction, he comments that after reading hundreds of diaries, he concluded among other things that "almost no one has had an easy life."[6] While reading, the thought struck me that I couldn't name a single acquaintance whom I have ever heard either complain or boast of an easy life. Mallon's right. Everybody can tell sad stories of life's injustices. And, truth to tell, they don't make most of us stronger than we would have been without them. Rather, life's slings and arrows have turned us into compromisers and cowards. Only the few rise through suffering to strength. Yet when you talk to the genuine achievers in almost any field, they attribute their success to the trials they endured. Artists, for example, are virtually unanimous in crediting their success to the obstacles they had to overcome and the creative problems they had to solve. They were forced to go beyond the predictable to more imaginative, courageous solutions. Robert Frost once commented that writing free (that is, unrhymed) verse is like playing tennis without a net. Not enough challenge to foster real creativity and growth.

But for us? We prefer the easy chair. An old Mankoff cartoon in the *Saturday Review* (4/12/80) tells it all. A weary man has just arrived home from work. He pours out his woes at the door to his wife. "What a day! First the car stalls going out of the driveway. Then my pen runs out of ink at work. And now I'm having some trouble opening this button on my coat." Life is hard.

Suffering—or at least the perception that life is much more difficult than it needs to be—is the universal lot of mankind. Some really do suffer (for example, victims of war or famine or injustice or poverty); others are equally certain they do, although objective observers might disagree with them. What distinguishes us from each other, then, is not the suffering, but the faithfulness *in spite of.*

A Man Called by God

In attempting to discern the essential elements in Joseph's rise to leadership, I have made it sound as if his success was all to Joseph's credit. Not true. I have left for last the most crucial factor: God's role in Joseph's extraordinary life. To fully understand him, we have to jump ahead to when the grain czar at last comes clean with his brothers. Until this point, he has been toying with them. "But Joseph said to them, 'Don't be afraid. Am I in the place of God? You intended to harm me, but God intended it for good to accomplish what is now being done, the saving of many lives'" (Genesis 50:19, 20). There it is, centuries before Paul's letter to the Romans: God has been working all along to bring good out of the evil you intended. Every step of the journey, whether languishing in prison or administering Pharaoh's kingdom, I have lived as a man called by God. He had a job for me to do. He was preparing me when we lived together with our father. My experiences in slavery, in Potiphar's service, in the dungeon, in Pharaoh's service—all came because "God intended it for good."

In other books, I have referred to England's William Wilberforce as one of my heroes. More than any other man, he was responsible for abolishing his country's abominable slave trade. In the course of his lifelong crusade, he incurred the wrath of politicians, business leaders, members of the royal family—in fact, the wrath of what seemed to be the overwhelming majority of England's influential people. Still he battled on, never giving up.

Not that he never wanted to. Fairly early in his perpetual campaign, he experienced a stunning setback in Parliament. He had made a little headway at this point. The House finally voted to abolish the trade "gradually." It wasn't much of a victory, but it was the closest Wilberforce had come to one, and it was close enough to give him some hope. Then even this tiny advance was pushed back when, across the English Channel, the fall of the Bastille in 1789 announced the people's revolution in France and sent panic into the hearts of Englishmen. By 1792, blood was flowing in the streets of Paris, and a frightened England reacted against any type of reform movement, including the movement to stop the slave trade.

It is not hard to imagine the depths of Wilberforce's disappointment. In the midst of his near despair, he turned for comfort to a letter from a dead friend, one he had already read dozens of times. He needed its strong medicine again. "My dear sir," it began,

> . . . unless the Divine power has raised you up to be as Athanasius contra mundum ["against the world"], I see not how you can go through your glorious enterprise, in opposing that execrable villainy, which is the scandal of religion, of England, and of human nature. Unless God has raised you up for this very thing, you will be worn out by the opposition of men and devils, but if God be for you who can be against you? Are all of them together stronger than God? Oh, be not weary of well-doing.

The letter was signed, "Your affectionate servant, John Wesley."[7] So Wilberforce persevered in his lonely campaign, introducing motions for abolition each year until, after forty years of dogged determination, he won the victory. Thanks to his persistence, Parliament abolished the slave trade in the British Empire. One man accomplished it. One man—and God.

"Unless God has raised you up. . . . "

So we return to Joseph, whose remarkable calling even Pharaoh could recognize. The king asked his court, "Can we find anyone like this man, one in whom is the spirit of God?" His words remind us of Nicodemus's insight regarding Jesus, that "no one could perform the miraculous signs you are doing if God were not with him" (John 3:2) No one has said it better than Paul in Romans 8:31: "If God is for us, who can be against us?"

In the final analysis, the secret of Joseph's success is no secret at all. When God calls people to do great things and they are willing to be God's instruments, who's able to stop them?

2

Guess Who's Coming to Dinner?

Genesis 42:1–45:15

What keeps drawing us back to familiar Bible stories is not a fascination with larger-than-life heroes. We outgrew our fixation on Superman, for example, before we left school. And on Santa Claus. Even the tooth fairy had to go (although the Lawson children pretended a faith they didn't have in order to keep the quarters coming). We have outgrown childish things; no more make-believe for us. Perhaps this impatience with the unreal explains our boredom (or irritation?) with politicians' empty promises.

No, we adults don't yearn for the fantastic. We inhabit a real world and we live in very real, often dysfunctional families. We turn to the Bible because there, in lives like Joseph's and families like Jacob's, we discover people who are quite similar to ourselves. God made something of them. We hope He will make something of us.

A Very Human Story

A Story of Betrayal

Joseph's problems—all too predictably—can be traced to his father. The sibling rivalry between the favored younger brother and his envious older brothers is no surprise. "Now Israel loved Joseph more than any of his other sons," Genesis 37:3 reports, "because he had been born to him in his old age; and he made a richly ornamented robe for him." A garment better than anything the doting father had given his older sons. The account doesn't tell us this, but it doesn't need to. The brothers concluded that Jacob (Israel) loved Joseph best, and they weren't wrong. Genesis 37:4 lays it out plainly: "When his brothers saw that their father loved him more than any of them, they hated him and could not speak a kind word to him."

It would have helped, of course, if Joseph had meekly deferred to them. He not only failed to do this but, adding insult to injury, he boasted of his superiority. "Listen to this dream I had," he demanded. Then he told of their sheaves bowing down to his, and "the sun and moon and eleven stars" (guess who?) kneeling before him. Not exactly tactful, this young Joseph. His crowing even got to his father, who "rebuked him and said, 'What is this dream you had? Will your mother and I and your brothers actually come and bow down to the ground before you?'" But that's all he said, or at least all that is recorded.

However, that's not all the brothers had to say, as you know, and it's not all they did. Reread their treacherous story in Genesis 37. It's not a pretty account, but it's a disturbingly human one.

A Story of Revenge

The deed was done and the boy was gone. However, the villainous brothers later learned that out of sight is not necessarily out of mind. Years later, when their country was famine stricken, Jacob dispatched his sons to deal with this erratic, unpredictable, but unquestionably powerful grain czar in Egypt. They found him strangely suspicious, but introduced themselves: "Your servants were twelve brothers, the sons of one man, who lives in the land of Canaan. The youngest is now with our father, and one is no more."

Joseph said to them, "It is just as I told you: You are spies! [*Where did this charge come from?* they had to be asking themselves. *What have we done or said that would lead this man to such an absurd conclusion?*] And this is how you will be tested: As surely as Pharaoh lives, you will not leave this place unless your youngest brother comes here. Send one of your number to get your brother; the rest of you will be kept in prison, so that your words may be tested to see if you are telling the truth. If you are not, then as surely as Pharaoh lives, you are spies!" (Genesis 42:13-16).

Then he clamped them into custody for three days.

For awhile, this very human story borders on the edge of cruelty. If Joseph had pursued his first thought—*I'll put all but one of you in prison and just send that one to fetch your youngest brother*—we would have sympathized with him. He had been brutally betrayed, after all, and vengeance is sweet. We'd have taken it, wouldn't we?

Even his second, much more lenient thought—*I'll keep one. The rest of you take grain and go get your brother*—still has a touch of retaliation in it. He withholds his identity, keeps them off balance, and toys with their emotions. The power is in his hands and he enjoys playing with it. His charade of not understanding, his trickery with the cup, his false accusations are to him harmless vents expelling long-repressed feelings. He will do his brothers no harm, but he will not rush to rescue them, either.

You can understand, can't you?

But it was Joseph who couldn't stand the pressure. He relented and reversed himself. Instead of sending just one brother back to Israel, he agreed to send all of them *but* one.

Even that was a scary proposition, however, because it meant persuading Jacob to let them take his current favorite,

Benjamin, away from his father. There was a certain irony in
the deal, though, that didn't escape the men: "Surely we are
being punished because of our brother. We saw how distressed
he was when he pleaded with us for his life, but we would not
listen; that's why this distress has come upon us" (Genesis
37:21). The ghost of Joseph haunted them still, even in Egypt.
And as in all such family quarrels, there is the plaintive protes-
tation of innocence. "Reuben replied, 'Didn't I tell you not to
sin against the boy? But you wouldn't listen! Now we must
give an accounting for his blood'" (37:22). How old are we, I
wonder, when we first learn those magical words, "It wasn't
my fault"? I can't remember when that wasn't my immediate,
instinctive answer to any accusation. Call it rationalization, call
it justification, call it explanation, or call it a downright lie, we
sincerely (or apparently sincerely) proclaim our innocence. Like
a latter-day Pilate, with vehemence we protest, "I am innocent
of this man's blood"—or of any other charge brought against
us.

As I said, it's a very human story.

A Story of Longing for Approval

Equally human is Joseph's longing for the approval of his
father. The man ordering Jacob's sons about is the second most
powerful person in Egypt, with a nation at his feet. He needs
nothing. His word is the law. Yet there is one person whose
approval he still seeks. "Tell my father about all the honor
accorded me in Egypt and about everything you have seen"
(Exodus 45:13). Tell my father I'm a success.

I have confessed that I don't know how early in life our
excuse-making begins; now I have to confess that I don't know
how old we are before we outgrow the need for our parents'
approval. I don't know because I'm not there yet. My father
died twenty years ago. One of my deepest regrets is that he
didn't live long enough to know about our new church building in Mesa, about my being a university president, about
how well his grandchildren turned out, about . . . about . . .

about . . . His opinion always mattered when he was living. It
still does.

It's a very human story, this one of Joseph and his father.

A Story of Separation and Reconciliation

When the brothers returned to their father to plead for
Benjamin to join them, Jacob's reaction was as selfish as always.
"You have deprived me of my children. Joseph is no more and
Simeon is no more, and now you want to take Benjamin.
Everything is against me" (Exodus 42:36). As if he is the only
member of the family who counts!

Reuben bravely shouldered the responsibility: "You may put
both of my sons to death if I do not bring him back to you.
Entrust him to my care, and I will bring him back" (42:37).

But even Reuben's generosity was not enough. Jacob was
adamant. "My son will not go down there with you; his brother
is dead and he is the only one left. [It must have been hard for
the other boys to hear themselves counted as nothing.] If harm
comes to him on the journey you are taking, you will bring my
gray head down to the grave in sorrow" (42:38). Period.

When the famine became severe enough, however, Jacob's
stubbornness finally yielded. When Joseph at long last saw his
younger brother Benjamin, he cried. His tears are the climax of
this narrative of separation and reconciliation. The shattered
family was reunited, the damage repaired.

This human story is as modern as right now, its parallels
acted out in stress-torn homes everywhere, although not often
with a happy ending. Relationships are easily ripped apart
and only repaired with difficulty—that is, with forgiveness,
with forgetfulness, with determination and grace. One that has
such an ending is Chris Carrier's. When he was ten years old,
Chris was abducted from his home in Coral Gables, Florida.
His kidnapper was furious with the boy's family over real or
imagined slights. He took his revenge out on Chris, burning
him with cigarettes and stabbing him numerous times with an
ice pick. Then he shot him in the head and discarded him in

the Everglades to die. As incredible as it seems, Chris survived, though he never recovered his sight in one eye. His kidnapper was never arrested.

Years later, a man confessed to the crime. He was David McAllister, an ex-convict living in a North Miami Beach nursing home. Now a frail seventy-seven-year-old, McAllister had carried his secret long enough. This man who had allegedly robbed a ten-year-old boy of sight in one eye was now blind himself.

Remarkably, Chris had not allowed his terrible childhood trauma to destroy his life. When he learned of McAllister's confession, he was serving as a youth minister. He went to see his former persecutor.

That first visit to his old enemy opened up an ongoing ministry. Chris visited him often, reading from the Bible and praying with him. His forgiving spirit led to McAllister's profession of faith in Christ.

There would be no arrest. The statute of limitations on the crime had run out long ago. Chris Carrier says, "While many people can't understand how I could forgive David McAllister, from my point of view I couldn't *not* forgive him. If I'd chosen to hate him all these years, or spent my life looking for revenge, then I wouldn't be the man I am today, the man my wife and children love, the man God has helped me to be."[8]

The parallel between Joseph's forgiveness of his brothers and Chris's forgiveness of his childhood tormentor is obvious, isn't it? Chris's grace compels us to a deeper reading of Joseph's experience. What we have been reading as a very human story must also be understood as a very godly story.

A Very Godly Story

Of course, people had trouble understanding Chris's willingness to forgive. To get even is human, to forgive is divine. In Joseph's forgiveness of his brothers, as in so many other elements of his adventures, we see the hand of God. This Genesis account reminds us of the prophet Hanani's words to Judah's King Asa: "For the eyes of the LORD range throughout the earth to strengthen those whose hearts are fully committed to him" (2 Chronicles 16:9). Joseph's heart did not waver; God matched his steadfastness with His own abiding strength.

A Story of Divine Guidance Through a Lifetime

It might not have always seemed that Joseph's God was with him, though. As his father's favorite, he must have felt like Browning's Pippa, that "God's in his heaven / all's right with the world." But as we have seen, his father's pampering of Joseph drove his brothers to desperation. When they sold him into slavery, did his confidence in God waver? Did he feel abandoned? How could he not have? Then when he was empowered to interpret his cellmates' dreams just as he had earlier explained his own dreams (with dire consequences) to his brothers, his promotion propelled him to the highest pinnacle of Egyptian authority. Even earlier, his service to Potiphar had to have made him the envy of others; until Potiphar's wife accused him of attempted seduction, he once again must have been feeling "all's right with the world," thanks to God.

What a wildly vacillating life—from favored son to betrayed brother; from favored servant to blackmailed prisoner; from the depths of the dungeon to the all-powerful grain czar of Egypt.

Joseph might have doubted God's providence at times, although there is no record that he did. What is certain is that the Scripture offers every assurance of God's guidance in Joseph's life, and the mature Joseph was completely confident that God had been in charge all along:

> And now, do not be distressed and do not be angry with yourselves for selling me here, because it was to save lives that God sent me ahead of you. For two years now there has been famine in the land, and for the next five years there will not be plowing and reaping. But God sent me

ahead of you to preserve for you a remnant on earth and
to save your lives by a great deliverance. So then, it was
not you who sent me here, but God. He made me father to
Pharaoh, lord of his entire household and ruler of all Egypt
(Genesis 45:5-8).

Joseph's confidence recalls Augustine's famous insight:
"God judged it better to bring good out of evil than to suffer no
evil to exist." In his wildly careening career, Joseph had seen
plenty of evil. But he also saw, at long last, the triumph of
good. I suspect Joseph would have agreed with Ralph Waldo
Emerson: "All I have seen teaches me to trust the Creator for all
I have not seen."

A number of years ago, I was impressed by Leslie Weatherhead's thoughtful insight into God's patient providence. He
pointed out in his *Wounded Spirits* that in 1665, hundreds of
good Christian people must have prayed for God to heal their
loved ones of the plague that was devastating England. But,
Weatherhead muses, if God had given the people what they
prayed for, vast portions of the population would still be peri-
odically wiped out by the plague. "Men would have put a
prayer in the slot and drawn out a cure," he observes. I have
reluctantly come to Weatherhead's conclusion. Prayer alone
leaves us dependent and demanding. Prayer plus research and
experimentation and plain hard work yields results that can
forever change things for the better.

So Joseph, languishing in slavery or imprisonment, could
not have known the rest of his story. But he could, and apparently did, rely on God to fulfill His plan.

A Story of Grace and Forgiveness

When reading the narrative of Joseph through Christian
eyes, it's impossible not to see something of a foreshadowing of
Christ, especially as we come to the end of the story. What
Joseph wants most of all is to have his family together again, as
did Jesus:

> My prayer is not for them alone. I pray also for those
> who will believe in me through their message, that all of
> them may be one, Father, just as you are in me and I am in
> you.... I in them and you in me. May they be brought to
> complete unity to let the world know that you sent me and
> have loved them even as you have loved me.... I have made
> you known to them, and will continue to make you known
> in order that the love you have for me may be in them and
> that I myself may be in them (John 17:20, 21, 23, 26).

Joseph, a good and just man, had been caring for all of
Egypt, but he saved his deepest affection for his family, unde-
serving though they might have been. Jesus came because God
loves all the world, but Jesus also has a special place in His
heart for those whom the Father has called to be with Jesus.
His grace and forgiveness are offered widely, but those who
accept it experience the grace and forgiveness in a way that
others do not.

One who experienced it to the fullest was Lois Cook. She
had been a member of our church in Mesa during most of my
twenty-year ministry there. When she let me know that she
had been diagnosed with cancer, I was heartbroken. Lois was
one of the quiet saints I have come to appreciate so much in the
church. These faithful ones demand so little, yet they are
always there, unobtrusively striving to grow more like the
Master, serving, giving, loving. I wasn't at all surprised when
just weeks before her death, she slipped me a piece of note-
paper. Her mind was already having difficulty focusing, so her
note is repetitious, incomplete, and not always coherent. But
there is no doubting her message:

1. I love my Lord
2. I love my four sons and their families
3. I was not a perfect mother but I was the was the best
mother I knew how how to be at my young age I was and
just hope they forgive they'll forgive they'll forgive my
shortcomings and remember the good times.

Her final wish was for God and her family to know of her love and, with that nagging sense of inadequacy that haunts most parents, to receive their grace and forgiveness in her dying hour. It's this universal need to forgive and be forgiven, to receive grace and extend it, that captivates us in the final scenes between Joseph and his family. We want everything to be all right between them, just as we yearn for the broken or bent relationships in our own family to be healed. And we know that such healing is impossible without grace and forgiveness.

An old Haggadic legend traces the origins of this healing balm clear back to the beginning of everything. "When God decided to create the world," the sages would say, "he said to Justice, 'Go and rule the earth which I am about to create.' But it did not work. God tried seven times to create a world ruled by Justice, but they were all failures and had to be destroyed. Finally, on the eighth try, God called in Mercy and said, 'Go, and together with Justice, rule the world that I am about to create, because a world ruled only by Justice cannot work.'" R.C. Lewontin, from whom I learned this tale, adds, "This time, apparently, it worked, more or less."[9] His "more or less" makes me smile. I like his honesty. You can't really say this world is working very well, even when mercy teams up with justice. They are both highly valued virtues. Unfortunately, we plead mercy for ourselves and demand justice for others. Not until our cry for mercy *for them* equals our pleas for ourselves will there be peace on earth—or at home.

So we turn with respect to Joseph's merciful dealings with his brothers. Such grace. Such magnanimity.

And we turn in awe to the cross to hear Jesus' plea for mercy —*for them*. There's something admirably human in our search for justice, but something graciously divine about Jesus' mercy.

A Story of Caring for a People

There is something special about Jacob's family. Certainly nothing in their behavior commends them; they are as dysfunctional as any family you know. Nor can we particularly admire

the patriarch. The wily young Jacob who cheated his brother
out of his birthright is now the wily old Jacob, still looking out
for himself first. What is special about Jacob and the family,
tribe, and nation descending from him can't be found in the
people but in the people's God. What is so remarkable about
their God is that, for reasons known best only to Him, He chose
Israel to be *His* people. Genesis is not primarily about Abraham,
Isaac, Jacob, and Jacob's progeny, but about their God and His
initiative in choosing and caring for His special family.

Having been a student of the Bible since my childhood, I
have often taken Israel's "chosenness" for granted. I am not
prepared, then, when I run across a prayer or poem that
assumes God's doesn't care about us. This anonymous Nahuatl
(ancient Mexican) poem, for example, presents a god as remote
from Israel's loving God as possible:

> Our Lord, Lord of the Ring,
> Self-engendered, self-willing, self-enjoying;
> Even as He wills, so shall He desire that it shall be.
> In the center of the palm of His hand He has placed us.
> He is moving us according to His pleasure.
> We are moving and turning like children's marbles,
> Tossed without direction.
> To him we are an object of diversion: He laughs at us.[10]

This bitter lament could not be farther from the psalmist's
praise, could it? Listen, for example, to this description of
God's love in Psalm 91:4.

> He will cover you with his feathers,
> and under his wings you will find refuge;
> his faithfulness will be your shield and rampart.

No cosmic cynicism here; no unsympathetic laughter, and
not some god making sport of human suffering. Instead, God
as father, as mother, as a bird protecting her chicks, as a never-
failing source of strength and security.

> For the Lord God is a sun and shield;
> the Lord bestows favor and honor;
> no good thing does he withhold
> from those whose walk is blameless.
> O Lord Almighty,
> blessed is the man who trusts in you (Psalm 84:11, 12).

During America's Civil War, President Abraham Lincoln, whose grasp of God's love still inspires, shared some of his thoughts about God in an often-reproduced letter to Mrs. Gurney. To Lincoln, God is a Power infinitely beyond yet intimately involved in the works of man.

> In all it has been your purpose to strengthen my reliance on God. I am much indebted to the good Christian people of the country for their constant prayers and consolations; and to no one of them more than to yourself. The purposes of the Almighty are perfect, and must prevail, though we erring mortals may fail to accurately perceive them in advance. We hoped for a happy termination of this terrible war long before this; but God knows best, and has ruled otherwise. We shall yet acknowledge his wisdom, and our own error therein. Meanwhile we must work earnestly in the best lights he gives us, trusting that so working well conduces to the great end he ordains. Surely he intends some great good to follow this mighty convulsion, which no mortal could make, and no mortal could stay.[11]

There is the difference between the Nahuatl believer and one who trusts in the God of the Bible: "Surely he intends some great good. . . ." In the heat of the Civil War, Lincoln anticipated goodness from God.

As did Joseph. As do we.

3

When You're Not So Sure You Want to Move

Genesis 45:16–47:12

No wonder Jacob refused at first to go down to Egypt. His boys had lied to him before. How could he be sure they weren't lying to him again? Genesis 45:26 says that they announced to Jacob: "'Joseph is still alive! In fact, he is ruler of all Egypt.' Jacob was stunned; he did not believe them." Not until they had "told him everything Joseph had said to them, and when he saw the carts Joseph had sent to carry him back," was he persuaded. "I'm convinced!" he finally said. "My son Joseph is still alive. I will go and see him before I die."

It wasn't just his skepticism he had to overcome. There was also the matter of his age. By this time, Jacob was very old. Traveling is hard enough for the young; for the aged, it can be life threatening. A journey of two hundred miles seems like nothing to twenty-first-century travel savvy Americans. But when your main mode of transportation is your feet, or, if you have means, aboard a donkey, you think twice before leaving your home territory for the speculative promises of another country. Old bones don't like long treks.

In spite of his earlier refusal to budge from Canaan, though, Jacob now set off with all his tribe. To see Joseph again and to stave off the famine's devastating effects were worth the tribulations of travel. As if to dispel any lingering doubts and to ensure a safe journey, he offered his sacrifices at Beersheba. God accepted them and offered Jacob assurance.

Jacob's Reluctance to Move

Just this morning, I had an extended telephone conversation with a good friend. Like Jacob, she has lived long and has many children. She continues to reside in the house she shared for a lifetime with her husband, who died several years ago. The house requires much attention, more than she is able to give it. Her children are stepping in, taking over, making decisions that she does not always approve of or appreciate. I asked her whether she had given any thought to moving into a retirement center. Such a move would, I added, simplify her life.

"Oh, no," she shot back. "I couldn't do that."

We dropped the subject. Of course she *could*, but she *would* not. There's a difference. She's comfortable in her old home. She can get around, be semi-independent, do her own shopping and housekeeping, and, in general, function quite well there, thank you.

I agree with her. She can. I'm not advocating a move. If I were in her shoes, I wouldn't leave either.

It's her immediate response, though, that makes me think of her as I reread this part of Jacob's story. Like her, he was in no mood to move. I have to confess that, like both of them, something in me has risen up to resist my every change of job or house. Moving day has always been threatening for reasons I can't always explain. I am not alone, either. Something there is that doesn't like a move, that wants us to stay put.

It will be true for the Israelites later on as well. After they have spent a few centuries in Egypt, they won't want to leave it. Now, though, and for very much the same emotional reasons, Jacob doesn't want to go near the place. He is held back by a very human fear of—we could soften it to "resistance to"—change. Rare is the person who, at Jacob's stage of life, is eager to change.

To be fair, however, we have to admit that Jacob has some justification for his hesitancy. He has reason to be afraid.

Jacob Was Afraid of the Egyptians

The Egyptians were powerful and the Israelites were not. And they are different, these Egyptians. Culturally more advanced, at least according to the Egyptians, they barely tolerate nomadic shepherds like these Israelites. Militarily, none can compare with Egypt, at least to Jacob's knowledge. To give up his safety far from Egypt's grasp and move his people onto Pharaoh's turf is a possibility Jacob does not want to entertain. And now that he has to, he doesn't like it.

We Americans identify with Jacob. With the attacks on the World Trade Center and the Pentagon in 2001, we experienced a fear of foreign powers that most U.S. citizens born after the 1960s had never felt. American wars are supposed to be fought somewhere else. The battleground is there, not here. Older Americans, though, remember when our country was very much afraid of the Russians. (Many of us recall laughing through the movie making fun of our fright, *The Russians Are Coming! The Russians Are Coming!*) After the September 11th terrorist attacks, commentators kept reminding us that we were now involved in a new kind of war, here on our soil but against an unknown enemy. During the Cold War, on the other hand, we knew exactly who our enemy was. The fear of that enemy was the most dominating characteristic of American life.

In 1949, for example, Archibald MacLeish commented that no country in the history of the world had been so intellectually and morally controlled by another people as we were by Russia during the four years following World War II. He exaggerated, perhaps, but not by much. He could have made the same statement in the 1960s and even later. To study post–World War II America is to learn that the strategy of our country's foreign policy was to take note of whatever the Russians were doing and then do the opposite. No politician dared say a kind word about the Russians; if he did, his defeat at the next election was certain. During President Kennedy's administration, we were even encouraged to build bomb shelters because we didn't know when or where communist missiles would attack.

Americans old enough to remember those post-war years often recalled them vividly and fearfully in the months following the terrorist attacks on New York and Washington, D.C. Because the terrorists were Middle Eastern Muslims, would American policy now be dictated by anti-Islamism as it was formerly dictated by anti-communism? Would Americans' freedoms be sacrificed to demands for guaranteed security from attack? Would fear of these latter-day Egyptians paralyze today's Jacobs?

Of course, Palestine was not then under attack by the Egyptians, but relations between Jacob's territory and that of his more powerful neighbor to the south had always been uneasy. The best defense was to keep a safe distance. Jacob knew this, yet now his sons wanted him to move to Egypt!

Jacob and his family were certainly concerned.

Jacob Was Concerned About Becoming Aliens

This was not an unreasonable fear, either. Joseph alludes to the grounds of their fear when he advises them:

> When Pharaoh calls you in and asks, "What is your occupation?" you should answer, "Your servants have tended livestock from our boyhood on, just as our fathers did." Then you will be allowed to settle in the region of Goshen, for all shepherds are detestable to the Egyptians (Genesis 46:33, 34).

Joseph's counsel always stops me when I read this passage. My grandfather was a shepherd. Admittedly, he was a gentleman shepherd, having studied pharmacology in college and worked for some years as a druggist before buying a sheep ranch in eastern Washington. One of my fondest childhood memories is of visiting his ranch. For a boy from Oregon's dairy country, this was a treat. I had no idea then that shepherds could be considered inferior to anyone. You have to be taught to look down on people; the thought never occurred to us children as we scampered among the sheep and their alert overseers. Besides, my grandfather was one of my idols. He still is. Thanks to him, I have always held shepherds in high esteem.

Mine would have been a minority opinion in the court of Pharaoh. Joseph was keenly aware of the majority's prejudice. He had undoubtedly quickly picked up on the Egyptian court's disdain for people like his family. He could protect Jacob, his brothers, and their families. He even had Pharaoh's approval in protecting them, but they were an exception. As a rule, shepherds were alienated from polite Egyptian society. The Israelites could shepherd their flocks on Egyptian soil, but only over there, in Goshen, away from polite society. In Egypt, they would be aliens.

"All shepherds." It's that little word *all* that lets the reader know Jacob's people were facing genuine prejudice. Whenever we pin a label on a race, a profession, a religion, a geographical area, or whatever and then blindly insist that "all" the people in that category are the same, we've moved from judgment to prejudgment, from the rational to the prejudicial.

The "all" here isn't a racially biased distinction; shepherds were detestable because they were different from the Egyptians. This dominant sense of "otherness" is sometimes missed in our discussions of racial prejudice. The Israelites were not going to be looked down on in Egypt because they were of a different race. "Difference," not "race," is what mattered.

Because race has played such a huge part in recent struggles for civil rights, we tend to think all such struggles are racial. "Black" versus "white" is the primary conflict in the United States because of this country's brutal early trade in African slaves. What is often overlooked, though, is a fact brought to light by African-American scholar Nathan Huggins, among others. He reminds us that on their own continent, Africans were hunting and capturing other Africans and selling them to Europeans. The Africans weren't thinking racially. They were just selling people different from themselves, who belonged to other tribes than their own. The distinctions of tribe were more real to them than race, which they shared with their captives. Modern whites cannot imagine how black persons could sell other black persons, but members of one tribe could easily distinguish their own "superior" tribe from other "inferior" ones, and those others were fair game.[12]

Think for a moment about what it means be different. All of us identify ourselves in a variety of ways: skin color, religion, education, vocation, neighborhood, income, spoken language, clothes, gender, sexual orientation, age, political party, sports teams, choice of newspapers or television programs, preference in music, and so on. And we all seek our own kind. When thrown into a situation in which we cannot quickly identify other people who share most of our traits, we feel alienated.

The heartache is what happens when alienation leads, as it so often does, to animosity. It's but a short step from one to the other. Once prejudice takes over, hatred gains the upper hand. You've probably heard the story—I don't know whether it's true, but I do know it could be—illustrating the hatred between Serbs and Croats in the 1990s intraracial genocide.

> One day, Franjo, a Croatian peasant, is working in his field when a voice from heaven calls out to him: "Franjo, you've been a good man. You work hard, you have true faith and integrity. Tell me what you want and you shall have it . . . with one little condition. Whatever I do for you,

I will do double for the Serb, Josip, who works the field
next to yours."

"I see," says Franjo, doffing his cap and scratching his
head. "Whatever you do for me, you'll do twice for that
Serbian? Very well, then, blind one of my eyes."[13]

Schadenfreude is the German word for Franjo's attitude, I
believe. It means "I rejoice in your misfortune." It's the curse
prejudice wishes on aliens. It's what the alienated believe
they—the powerful, the native, the ones in charge of the
culture—are laughing about. It's what Jacob feared. (We'll take
a closer look at this disturbing subject of prejudice in the next
chapter.)

Jacob Was Concerned About Family Tensions

I may be pushing it here, but if I'd been in Jacob's patriar-
chal shoes, I wonder how eager I would have been to take off
for Egypt in the company of my squabbling, unreliable sons
and their sprawling families. Not that Jacob could blame his
family problems on anybody but himself. His open favoritism
toward Joseph in the beginning set the brothers against one
another. They long ago learned not to expect impartiality from
their father. (By this time, though, the other brothers were in no
position to protest, since Joseph was taking good care of all of
them.)

It would be surprising if it were not so common, by the way,
to find Joseph perpetuating this partiality in his treatment of
Benjamin, his mother's son and his only full brother. Genesis
45:21 says, "Joseph gave them carts, as Pharaoh had commanded, and he also gave them provisions for their journey. To each
of them he gave new clothing, but to Benjamin he gave three
hundred shekels of silver and five sets of clothes."

Did Joseph suspect that favoring Benjamin would set off
another round of hostility among the brothers? "Then he sent
his brothers away, and as they were leaving he said to them,
'Don't quarrel on the way!'"

The tension within the family had to be pretty severe as they moved closer to Egypt and the coming reunion of Jacob and Joseph. The whole truth of the brothers' duplicity was bound to come out. Jacob would now learn how deceitful his sons had been. He would now know how they made up the story of the wild animal that had attacked the boy and left behind only his bloodstained robe. He would catch on that they had been living a lie all these years.

There had to be the usual grumbling. If Jacob was loathe to leave, he was not alone. You can't have a family that big without a good number of them complaining about the hassles of packing up, the hardships along the way, the uncertain future, the unfairness of it all.

Jacob Was Concerned About Being Old

I mentioned this earlier, but there is a little more to say about Jacob's age. As has been wisely pointed out, the great danger in the first phase of life is not to take a risk. Early childhood growth is all about risk-taking, going where you've never been before, trying what is strange, inviting failure and embarrassment but then trying again anyway. In the last phase of life, the danger is even greater. We have learned to protect ourselves, to avoid risk whenever possible—to our detriment. I doubt Jacob could ever have been persuaded to leave Canaan if the famine hadn't been so severe and the promise of seeing his long-lost son hadn't been so compelling. Finally, he summoned his strength to go. He was very old, but he wasn't finished.

One of the most courageous women I have ever heard of, Helen Keller, long ago inspired me with her observation, "Life is either a daring adventure or nothing at all." When I first read this statement, I thought it was for the young—a challenge to them to be up and doing, stretching and daring, growing and developing. And perhaps it was. But now that I am no longer young, I believe it is even more appropriate counsel for older people. For us, the choice is to dare or decline. Our options are not always as stark as Jacob's, but they are as inevitable. The high cost of refusing to move, of resisting change, of failure to venture forth, is to grow stagnant. Stagnation is where dying begins.

So daring to change is essential at any age. Having served so long in church ministries and college and university administration, my greatest challenge over the years has been to lead people through the traumas of change. Always they resist, at least at first. Their resistance is often expressed by questioning the leader's motives or judgment or even his personal morality. They are not bad people, these resistors. They just don't want to go where they haven't been before. James Lee Witt, director of the Federal Emergency Management Agency during the Clinton administration, imaginatively disarmed his opponents by displaying a paper in his office on which he had written, "When entering this room, do not say 'We've never done it this way before.'" I wonder why I never thought of doing the same thing.

Insisting on always doing what we've always done in the way we've always done it is the kiss of death for an organization, any organization. Witt's job was to lead his agency in nearly superhuman recovery efforts in the aftermath of floods, hurricanes, and other disasters. Rescue operations can't always be conducted by the book because books can't anticipate all the exigencies of crises. No two crises are the same. Witt's warning was wise advice. People who protest, "We've never done it this way before" have seldom thought their objection through to its logical conclusion: If they only do what they've already done, how will they ever do anything new?

Jacob's hesitation has had us probing the possible sources of his reluctance. We've looked at just a few. The truth is, the fear could be almost anything. It doesn't take much to convince us to stand pat. We humanly prefer the misery we know to the possibilities we don't know.

I mentioned the inspirational Helen Keller, who, though deaf and blind, would not let her handicaps intimidate her. Another hero of my youth was Theodore Roosevelt, who, like me, battled asthma as a youth. He never knew when an attack would hit, leaving him gasping for every breath, turning many and many a night into a wakened nightmare. When he was in college, a physician warned him that he had serious heart trouble. (I had also been alerted as a child that chronic asthma often leads to a weakened heart.) He should live a quiet, sedate life, he was told. He must not overly task his heart. But young Teddy took the opposite tack. In defiance of his medical advisors, he vowed to live the strenuous life. If they said that he shouldn't do it, he did it. Pursuing his vow eventually led him to the White House. His courage inspired many young people to live more fully in spite of less than robust health.

Many years later, with my youth far behind me, I read Marian Wright Edelman's observation of Dr. Martin Luther King. Like most Americans, she admired him as a great leader, but what she admired in addition, she said, was his admission of how often he was afraid and uncertain of his next step. He had the ability, like many other African-American adults, she thought, to make "a way out of no way."[14] In his own writings, Dr. King made it clear that there wouldn't have been a way if God hadn't opened it up for him.

Jacob would have said the same thing.

That's why we also must read this story from God's point of view.

Jacob's Reluctance Was Changed to Resolve

So far we've been concentrating on Jacob's reluctance to relocate his extended family in Egypt. The fact is, of course, that he did it anyway. He overcame his resistance. Driven by the famine and drawn by Joseph, Jacob's resolve was bolstered by God's promise. He set out on this journey he dreaded.

In an earlier famine, God had specifically told Jacob's father Isaac not to "go down to Egypt" (Genesis 26:2). Instead, He said, "Stay in this land for a while, and I will be with you and will bless you." Isaac did what the Lord told him. I mention this event here only to underscore the fact that God's instructions are not always the same. Earlier, going to Egypt was not the solution; this time, it was. Walking with God means being alert to His ongoing guidance.

> And God spoke to Israel in a vision at night and said, "Jacob! Jacob!"
> "Here I am," he replied.
> "I am God, the God of your father," he said. "Do not be afraid to go down to Egypt, for I will make you into a great nation there. I will go down to Egypt with you, and I will surely bring you back again. And Joseph's own hand will close your eyes" (Genesis 46:1-3).

This story, you see, is not just about Jacob and Joseph, or Joseph and his brothers, or Joseph and Pharaoh, or even Jacob and his descendants. It's about God and His leading. Jacob's twofold motivation is simple: escape famine, reunite with Joseph. God's purpose is much larger: build a great nation. Because it is *His* purpose, the nation will be built. Therefore, Jacob has nothing to fear. God will bring His plan to completion.

God's Promise to Jacob

This theme of nation building was not new with Jacob. God's first promise was to Abraham (see Genesis 12:1, 2). He repeated it to Isaac (Genesis 26:3-5). And now He confirmed it with Jacob. "I will make you into a great nation" (46:3, 4). This time God added a new detail to an old promise made at Bethel, namely that the growth of Jacob's descendants into a nation would take place in Egypt. They might have been just a band of shepherds in the eyes of the Egyptians (and, it goes without saying, in their own eyes), but God was working through them to fulfill His promises.

So they departed for Egypt, where Joseph had already reassured Pharaoh they would be willing to be shepherds. They would not be asking for special favors as Joseph's relatives. They ended up, nevertheless, with the best land.

Reading this story in today's supercharged political climate helps explain the ongoing tensions in the Middle East, doesn't it? Three great religions accept Genesis as Scripture. Judaism, Islam, and Christianity trace their heritage to Abraham. Muslims read the account with different eyes, since they trace their lineage through Abraham's son Ishmael rather than Isaac. Jews and Christians trace their line back through Jacob to Abraham. Jacob's anxiety lest he not be buried in the land of his fathers presages modern Israel's passion for a land of their own and Palestinian insistence that this holy land is theirs by right of inheritance. Today's Western conflict with Islamic terrorism and the attending fears of *them* that haunt both sides is only the latest chapter in the conflicts that Genesis records.

Scholars read God's promise to make Israel a great nation with curiosity. What did God mean? Great in what way? Numerically? Militarily? Intellectually? Morally and spiritually? If they can answer these questions, they may be able to offer some hope for a peaceful settlement in the Middle East. If they can't, there will be no end to the making of war there.

Jacob, of course, did not ask such questions. He simply heard God's promise and acted on it. He went to Egypt.

Jacob's Confidence in God

And Jacob went with renewed confidence. He had God's word. He and his family would be safe. Egypt was still Egypt, and they were but shepherds, but there was nothing to fear. God said so.

It's amazing what a difference trust makes—how much you can accomplish if you just believe you can. I almost wrote "what a difference self-confidence makes." It would have been an accurate statement. Self-confidence makes an enormous difference. But Jacob's resolution wasn't based on his ability alone. His was God-confidence. Someone else would be his security.

Many years later, Jacob's descendant David expressed this God-confidence in music. He, too, knew something of facing overwhelming odds, of having to summon courage from somewhere to go on. He found his strength in God:

> The Lord is my light and my salvation—
>   whom shall I fear?
> The Lord is the stronghold of my life—
>   of whom shall I be afraid?
> When evil men advance against me to devour my flesh,
>   when my enemies and my foes attack me,
>   they will stumble and fall.
> Though an army besiege me,
>   my heart will not fear;
>   though war break out against me,
>   even then will I be confident (Psalm 27:1-3).

For him, as for Jacob, boldness came from following the Lord: "Guide me in your truth, and teach me; for you are God my Savior" (Psalm 25:5).

The difference between self-confidence and God-confidence is aptly illustrated by something discovered during the building of the Golden Gate Bridge. If you drive to San Francisco from the north along the coastal highway, you have to cross the legendary bridge to get over the mouth of the bay. Under construction between 1933 and 1937, the building at first progressed slowly and dangerously. Over a dozen men died in the first couple of years, some plummeting as much as seven hundred feet to their deaths in the waters below. At last the work ceased. Something had to be done. This loss of life could not go on. A solution was found and, during the shutdown, workers stretched a mammoth safety net costing several hundred thousand dollars (a huge amount then) under the bridge. Then the work began again. In the remaining years of construction, six more people fell but that safety net saved their lives. In addition, efficiency on the project increased by 25 percent.

A predictable consequence, don't you think? When you

aren't afraid of dying, you can work with greater efficiency. What interests me in this bit of history is this: The pre-net workers were the same men as the post-net men. Same skills. Same confidence in their skills. The increased efficiency came not from greater self-confidence, but from "net-confidence." The source of their safety was outside themselves.

As it was with Jacob. And with us.

4
Construction Production

Exodus 1:1-22

This chapter, I should warn you at the outset, is about prejudice. And because it is about prejudice, it must also be about ignorance, fear, oppression and slavery, suffering, and, finally, murder. It won't be light reading. We may prefer smiling at our prejudices—with W.C. Fields, for example, who famously quipped, "I am free of all prejudices. I hate everybody equally" —but we have to admit there is really nothing to smile about when they take charge.

I'm afraid it won't be inspiring reading, either. We'll be studying our own and our culture's pet biases and we won't like what we see. I hope you'll stay with me even though we would rather avoid the subject if we could.

A New Pharaoh in Egypt

When Israel first settled down in Egypt, things looked good. A generous-hearted Pharaoh, out of gratitude for Joseph's brilliant work, welcomed the whole family of Jacob, seventy in all. He offered them refuge from the biting famine. He granted the tribe of shepherds leave to graze their flocks in Egypt's prime pastures. The estranged brothers were reconciled, the reunion of the father and his long-thought-dead son was consummated, and there was great rejoicing.

But the shadow of prejudice was visible even then as the settling in began. Quietly, but ominously, the Bible mentions it: "for all shepherds are detestable to the Egyptians" (Genesis 46:34). Ah, they could move onto the rich fields of Goshen—not necessarily because that was best for the sheep, but because it was comfortably distant from the more urbanized Egyptians and their farming cousins.

It was not an overwhelming problem for the Israelites at first, this Egyptian disdain for shepherds and their smelly flocks, not as long as there was a Pharaoh on the throne who remembered how their kinsman Joseph saved the nation from famine. Gratitude overcomes prejudice as long as memory holds. But it didn't last long. In Exodus 1, "a new king, who did not know about Joseph, came to power in Egypt." He didn't know about Joseph, but he did know about Joseph's people. And what he knew was that there were now too many of them in Egypt.

> "Look," he said to his people, "the Israelites have become much too numerous for us. Come, we must deal shrewdly with them or they will become even more numerous and, if war breaks out, will join our enemies, fight against us and leave the country" (Exodus 1:9, 10).

Thus it began—the struggle between a frightened ruler and the ruled people whose very numbers scared him. If you were a betting person, your money would have been on Pharaoh. Who could have ever dreamed that with all his wealth, authority, manpower, and weaponry, he would eventually prove helpless against a poor, powerless, initially leaderless, weaponless bunch of slaves, no matter how many there were of them?

Pharaoh's Prejudice Toward the Israelites

As I said, our assignment in this chapter is to look hard at the root of the conflict that will eventually lead to Israel's liberation. We start, not with the conflict itself, but with the eyes of Pharaoh. Eyesight is his problem. He can't clearly see what he is looking at. In a real sense, the showdown is between eyes that will not see the Israelites for who they are, and the eyes of God, which never leave the Israelites—eyes that see their mistreatment, eyes that want to see their eventual release and resettlement in a land of their own, that "flowing with milk and honey" land of Canaan.

Pharaoh didn't despise the Israelites personally. He probably didn't even know any firsthand. Kings don't normally hang out with serfs. They didn't upset him as long as they were tending their sheep, keeping quiet, staying in their "place." What worried him was that, with their rapidly growing numbers, they might move out of their place—and move him out of his! The more numerous they became, the more precarious his hold was over them.

An American History of Prejudice

The parallel to language we used to hear about African-Americans in the United States is too obvious to ignore, isn't it? How often my generation was told in our youth that black people were just fine "in their place." Their place was never explicitly described to us, but it wasn't hard to figure out that it was somewhere other than, or somewhere quite below, that of the white man's place. Slavery was out, of course (unlike Pharaoh's solution for the Israelites), but confinement to place was in.

We Americans can find little solace in our nation's sordid history of prejudice. Even our esteemed founding fathers looked on others through its distorting lenses. For most of us, Thomas Jefferson represents all that was noble and idealistic in our country's struggle for independence. This is the man who wrote in the Declaration of Independence that "all men are created equal." Since the nation's founding, though, generations of Americans have fought over the meaning of those simple words, the arguments leading to a brutal civil war in the nineteenth century and the sometimes vicious civil rights battles of the twentieth century. That it has taken us so long to grant equality to all Americans should not be surprising when we consider that the author of those words did not really believe them. His prejudice blinded him to their truth. He really meant that only white men (and not even white women) were created equal. Of the nation's slaves he once wrote, "Negroes have a very strong and disagreeable odor. They seem to require less sleep. Their love is ardent but it kindles the senses only, not the imagination. In reason they are much inferior to whites; in imagination, they are dull, tasteless and anomalous. Their griefs are transient."[15] How startling it has been for modern students of American history to learn that most of our founding fathers agreed with Jefferson. They didn't intend for Africans to enjoy the independence they demanded for themselves.

They held similar views regarding Native Americans. They could tolerate Native Americans as long as they stayed in their place. Their place was a very low one, so low that the white man could appropriate their land at will.

Jefferson's arrogant dismissal of "Negroes" made me think of Robert Ringer's explanation of the word *barbarian*. He says it came from the Sanskrit, where it translates as "stammerer." In other words, "if a person didn't speak your language and act like you, he was a stammerer—an ignoramus."[16] But that reasoning begs the question, doesn't it? Who is the ignoramus— the stammerer or the one who can't understand him? Jefferson was very quick to "explain" the "Negro's" inferiority to his own satisfaction, but time has proved him wrong on all points. Who is the stammerer?

The Reasoning Behind Prejudice

What is so seductive about prejudice is its economy of thought. You don't have to spend much time thinking about people if you have already labeled and rated them. Everybody who wears the same label bears the same stigma. Therefore, all Israelites are dumb shepherds. All Egyptians are superior people. All African-Americans are inferior to whites. All _____ are _____. You fill in the blanks. The lazy mind, once these tags are attached and the varieties of humanity are sorted into their assigned categories, shuts down. So all Middle Easterners are suspect since September 11, all Muslims are to be feared, all Palestinians are treacherous, all Israelis are murderous toward Palestinians, all Americans are patriotic and pure.

And, of course, everybody else is prejudiced. As I said, you fill in the blanks.

Even when we try not to be biased, we are. Our measuring rod is always personal. I compare all others to me. To the extent they are like me, they are all right; the greater the differences between them and me, the harder it is for me to find reassuring similarities, and the more difficult it is to love them as myself as Jesus would have me do (Matthew 22:39). Pharaoh clearly could see no likenesses between the despised Israelites and his own kind. He could have benefited from Jesus' insight into the spiritual advantage the child has over us adults: "I tell you the truth, unless you change and become like little children, you will never enter the kingdom of heaven" (Matthew 18:3).

Whole books have been written about this verse. Becoming like children is one of the great challenges for spiritual growth. How do we become like children? Well, for one thing, little children are not naturally prejudiced. They have to be taught to discriminate, to see the distinctions the adults in their lives have mastered.

One of my favorite examples of this native childlike fairness—whether spoken by a child or an adult who had retained (or relearned) the childlike spirit, I don't know—is that of the Samoan who reproved a Polynesian child for teasing a Negro: "You must not despise him because his skin is black. His soul is as brown as yours and mine."[17] (The story has been around a long time, as you can tell by the use of "Negro" in place of "African-American" or "black.")

The Samoan had found the common meeting ground for persons of all color—the soul. This writer, even trying to be unbiased, would naturally have said, "as white. . . ." The wisdom is in subordinating color, "difference," to soul, "what we have in common."

Pharaoh was ignorant of the concept.

Pharaoh's Ignorance of the Israelite's History

This failure to see what was common among Egyptians and Israelites wasn't the only example of Pharaoh's ignorance. That this king didn't know about Joseph is not surprising. Jacob's descendants had been in Egypt for a long time. Pharaoh would have known his people's history well. Official memory is nurtured and carefully passed down from generation to generation. As has often been pointed out, though, history is written by the victors, not the vanquished. He would have known of his regal ancestors; he might even have been aware of the great famine that brought Joseph to prominence. But the credit for rescuing Egypt from the ravages of hunger would have gone to the ruling king, not his grain czar, whose name was dropped from the official records. Schoolchildren in America memorize the names of the nation's presidents; they usually can't name a single secretary of agriculture.

So Egypt's indebtedness to the Israelites' ancestor Joseph was lost in the mists of time. Lost also, of course, were any sense of gratitude and any curiosity to get to know these slaves as persons. Ignorant of the truth of the Israelites' role in Egypt's history, Pharaoh could give prejudice free rein.

A History of Willful Ignorance
The histories of Jews and Christians offer too many examples of this almost willful ignorance. In the early days of

Christianity, the new believers in Jesus were scorned and often persecuted. Their tormentors were Jews and Gentiles alike. In the New Testament, Jewish leaders hunted down these Christ-believers. (See the early career of the apostle Paul who, as Saul of Tarsus, led the charge against the Christians.) Just a couple of centuries later, however, the tables were turned. By the time of Constantine, who made Christianity the official religion of the Roman Empire, Christians either forgot their earlier mistreatment by the Jews or, even worse, determined to get even. They turned against the Jews and persecuted them viciously. The noted German theologian Hans Kung says Jews were "slaughtered in Western Europe during the first three Crusades and Jews in Palestine were exterminated." Even into the twentieth century, the Jews were hunted and, during the murderous Nazi regime, six million of them were eradicated. I can hardly take it in that much earlier, according to Kung:

> Three hundred Jewish communities were destroyed in the German Empire from 1348 to 1349; Jews were expelled from England (1290), France (1394), Spain (1492) and Portugal (1497). Later came the horrifyingly virulent anti-Jewish speeches of the elderly Luther. Persecution of Jews continued after the Reformation, there were pogroms in Eastern Europe, and so on. It must be admitted that, during these periods, the Church probably slew more martyrs than it produced. All of which is incomprehensible to the modern Christian.[18]

Equally incomprehensible to me is that in modern Israel's treatment of Palestinians, it sometimes seems to an outsider that the Israelis might have forgotten their own earlier centuries of suffering.

If you do not know or choose to remain ignorant of your own history, and if you will not consider your enemy's side of the story, prejudice will triumph.

Pharaoh's Fear of the Israelites

Pharaoh's fear was that "they will become even more numerous and, if war breaks out, will join our enemies, fight against us and leave the country" (Exodus 1:10). This seems a reasonable concern, doesn't it? Their numbers were large, their hostility toward their Egyptian masters quite evident, and their readiness to ally themselves with Egypt's enemies a foregone conclusion. On first reading this section, we agree with the king. He had a point.

On second reading, however, we would like to suggest to the king something he had overlooked. Was the Israelites' alliance with his enemies a foregone conclusion? Isn't it conceivable that, treated right, they would side with Egypt? Look at the history of the African in America, for example. During the War between the States, many Southern slaves willingly fought for the South. During World War I and World War II, they voluntarily fought for America, even though their grievances against their country were numerous.

Wouldn't it have been possible, Your Majesty, to reach an equitable compromise with the Israelites, to defuse their hostility and win their allegiance? With a little different kind of treatment, couldn't these potential enemies become allies?

I know, I know. I'm reading too much into the story from the vantage point of my own time. Such thinking would never have occurred to the all-powerful king. But as a result of his obtuseness, reasonableness receded and fear took over.

When fear reigns, even the most absurd thinking seems reasonable. Here's an example you may have a little trouble believing. When William Howard Taft was president, Mrs. Taft once demanded that head usher Ike Hoover fire a new White House usher. He had just hired him that morning. He did as he was told; he let the man go. He had served five presidential couples and did not expect them to be reasonable.

Apparently Mrs. Taft did not explain herself to Ike, but she later did to her personal maid, Maggie.

"They're bad luck, that's what they are. Won't have them in my White House."

"Ma'am?" Maggie asked.

"In the Philippines, we had a bald-headed servant with a beard. Tropical storm almost swept the palace out to sea, and us with it. . . ."

"You don't say, ma'am."

"And another time, in Cuba, where Mr. Taft had gone to put down the revolution. . . . There were bearded staff members there and the Marines had to rescue us from the rebels. I will not permit that kind of jinx to follow us into the White House."[19]

You probably had to read this dialogue more than once to make sense of it. Even then, it didn't make sense, did it? No, but it is a good illustration of what passes for reason among the severely biased. Mrs. Taft believed she was making very good sense. That's the trouble with all such prejudice. It seems so reasonable and is so very hard to refute.

There was at least an economic explanation for Pharaoh's fear. As I will repeatedly be reminding us, these despised Israelites provided the manpower to run the economy. Hated as they were, the government couldn't function without their labor. If they were to leave the country, as Pharaoh feared, there would be a huge social upheaval. How would Pharaoh ever be able to replace such cheap labor? He relied on the Israelites with a dependency that engenders hatred. We naturally despise the ones we can't function without—as we fear the ones we hate.

Pharaoh's Response to the Israelites

Oppression and Slavery

"So they put slave masters over them to oppress them with forced labor, and they built Pithom and Rameses as store cities for Pharaoh" (Exodus 1:11). From independent shepherds to forced laborers. It was a terrible comedown for Jacob's family. Once God's people, they were now government property. The verb says it all: "to *oppress* them." It is reminiscent of Abraham Lincoln's scathing attack on slavery in America. He bemoaned the mentality of owners who viewed their slaves as mere property and nothing more. To protect their property, they went into politics "to insist upon all that will favorably affect its value as property, to demand laws and institutions and a public policy that shall increase and secure its value, and make it durable, lasting, and universal. The effect on the minds of the owners is to persuade them that there is no wrong in it."[20] Nothing wrong with reducing human beings to economic assets, interchangeable parts in the machinery of business, but not real persons who cry real tears and whose hearts beat with real human longings.

Pharaoh's overseers "worked them ruthlessly. They made their lives bitter with hard labor in brick and mortar and with all kinds of work in the fields; in all their hard labor the Egyptians used them ruthlessly" (Exodus 1:13, 14).

I wish we could treat this story of Israel in Egypt as an historical exception. It would be much more bearable if we could read of Pharaoh's atrocities, sympathize with the battered Israelites, and then thank God that such barbarous behavior was behind us—that it happened in a cruder, less civilized age but that we moderns have outgrown such things.

I wish that we weren't reading in today's newspapers about the ongoing war against terrorism, about Pakistanis and Indians killing each other over disputed Kashmir, about the never-ending Palestinian-Israeli war, about tribal hatreds in Afghanistan, about . . . about . . . about . . .

I wish that Europe hadn't been torn apart in the 1990s by ethnic cleansing and genocide in the former Yugoslavian territories. I wish I hadn't read in a *Time* article entitled "Atrocity and Outrage" of the skeletal figures behind barbed wire, murdered babies in a bus, and two-and-a-half million people driven from their homes into detention camps "in an orgy of 'ethnic cleansing.'" J.F.O. McAllister, who wrote the article, seemed to have the same difficulty taking it in as I did. "Surely these pictures and stories come from another time—the Dark Ages, the Thirty Years' War, Hitler's heyday," he writes. Then he adds:

> But the evidence, accumulating for months, is now inescapable: like an addiction, hatred is consuming the people who used to call themselves Yugoslavs. Every throat slit makes someone else thirst for blood. "They killed my husband and son," says a tearful Bosnian refugee. "They burned our home. But they can never rest easy, because one day we will do the same to them, or worse. My children will get their revenge, or their children." No one anywhere can pretend any longer not to know what barbarity has engulfed the people of the former Yugoslavia.[21]

The UN's outgoing man in Sarajevo, General Lewis MacKenzie, was asked, "You have had nine peacekeeping tours in places like Gaza, Nicaragua, and Cyprus. How does this compare?" His response:

> You can take the hate from all those previous tours and multiply by 10. I've never seen anything close to that. Even if only 10 percent of what each side accuses the other of doing is true, in the minds of the people it has grown to horrendous proportions. If the leadership said, "O.K., let's sit down and sort this thing out," I'm not sure whether people would accept that because there is so much hate for the other side. Really deep, gut-wrenching hate. Once you start calling them baby killers, pregnant-women killers, and talk about cooking babies, those are not good grounds for negotiations.[22]

Obviously, we can't treat Israel's descent into oppressive slavery as some kind of historic exception to the rule. No, the rule is oppression. Freedom is the exception. This is why free men and women like you and me can't take this period of Israel's history lightly. It is why African-Americans, in the darkest days of slavery in this nation, turned for inspiration to Israel's miserable sojourn in and subsequent delivery from Egypt. Israel's woes were their woes, Israel's hope their hope.

The protection of freedom demands diligence because it is so fragile. If a favored people like Jacob's family can so quickly fall from Goshen's plains to Egypt's brickyards, anybody can. If prejudice can so violently turn people into property, then rational compassion must do everything in its power to protect them. If political power determines to subjugate a weak segment of society, then love must claim that segment as neighbors and love them back to personhood and protect them from oppression.

Murder Their Firstborn Sons

Hitler called the extinction of European Jews "the final solution." Murder is the inevitable consequence of prejudice run amok. When General Philip Sheridan muttered, "The only good Indians I ever saw were dead," he probably meant it. Prejudice gave him permission to consign a race to oblivion. It is not much different from Pharaoh's order regarding Hebrew births: "If it is a boy, kill him; but if it is a girl, let her live."

If you are going to wipe out your enemies, it's best to do it while they are young and helpless.

This is prejudice's ultimate and final solution.

Transforming Prejudice

I can't close this chapter on such a dour note. I have made it sound as if Pharaoh's attitude is inevitable, as if people will always hate those who are not like them. Not true. If that were so, Jesus' command coupling love of God with love of neighbor would be only so many empty words. But they aren't empty words. People can learn to love each other, to forgive their enemies, to care for the less fortunate, to break down the dividing walls of hostility, to outgrow their own prejudices. Egyptian and Israelite can live at peace on the same land.

Let me give you just one instance of overcoming. I could tell you many more, but this chapter has run out of space.

Let me take you back to the 1960s to a Baptist institution in Georgia by the name of Mercer University. Something happened that forced Mercer to face up to the consequences of its own teaching. Many years earlier, one of the school's alumni, Harris Mobley, had gone to Africa as a missionary. His ministry there was successful. Among others, he converted a young Ghanaian named Sam Jerry Oni. An admirer of his missionary mentor, Oni applied to study at Mobley's alma mater. But in one of American Christianity's ironies, Mercer University, which prepared missionaries for the rest of the world, did not admit persons of black skin. When the school received Sam Jerry Oni's application, a debate erupted. This was in the earliest days of the civil rights struggle, before such debates became commonplace—and often violent. At Mercer, antiacceptance forces (those who believed Oni should be denied admission) demanded the university remain true to its all-white heritage. Proacceptance forces were equally vocal in warning that the whole missions program was at risk. They also insisted they had no choice if they believed the Christian ethic. Their arguments prevailed. Long before it seemed the reasonable thing to do in the conservative South, Mercer courageously admitted Sam Jerry Oni. The next logical step was also taken. Mercer dropped racial barriers for African-Americans as well. *Reader's Digest,* reporting this good news, added, "So the missionary work came full cycle."[23]

Maybe our study of this passage can be called inspirational after all. If it leads us, as Mercer was led, to eliminate prejudice and treat all people with the love of God and the mercy of Christ, we'll have come a little closer to the kind of spiritual worship the apostle Paul commends. "Do not conform any longer to the pattern of this world," he urges us, "but be transformed by the renewing of your mind." In so doing, we "will be able to test and approve what God's will is—his good, pleasing and perfect will" (Romans 12:2).

Prejudice is the pattern of this world, but minds closed by prejudice can be transformed.

And these renewed minds can follow God's good, pleasing, and perfect will.

I find the prospect inspiring, don't you?

5

Called Out
of Hiding

Exodus 2:1-25

Moses is now considered one of history's greatest leaders, but he didn't seem so in the beginning. Since we know the whole story, we quickly name Moses whenever we're asked to name an ideal leader. His contemporaries wouldn't have thought so, though, at least when he was young. To some of them, he was a hot-tempered bully. To others, he probably seemed little more than a pampered palace dandy. And after he fled Egypt, when he was a refugee tending sheep, nobody would have pictured him as a national leader.

Some Unlikely Leaders

From Moses' early years, you can easily see that God had some work to do on him. He resembles some of the unlikely presidents who have served during the last several decades: a humble Missouri haberdasher, Harry S. Truman; a spoiled rich kid, John F. Kennedy; a Georgia peanut farmer, Jimmy Carter; a clumsy ex-football player, Jerry Ford; a B-movie actor, Ronald Reagan; an undisciplined Casanova, Bill Clinton; an underestimated Texas entrepreneur, George W. Bush. In fact, when you look at the whole list of presidents beginning with Franklin D. Roosevelt, only Roosevelt, Dwight Eisenhower, Lyndon Johnson (should I add Richard Nixon?), and the first George Bush seemed qualified for the office before they stepped into it. Some proved less than brilliant leaders, such as Carter and Ford, and others less than noble, like Nixon and Clinton. But the one who kept surprising people was Ronald Reagan. Even now, several presidencies after his retirement, the reappraisal of Reagan's impact on America continues, with the man rising higher in most historians' estimation. That reappraisal began early. Back in 1984, toward the end of his first term, Hugh Sidey wrote of the sitting president:

> There were probably as many facts known about Reagan's life and career when he took office as any recent President's. Yet we are just now realizing that Reagan was almost incidentally a sportscaster, movie actor and television personality. From his early days in Dixon, Illinois, Reagan has been a leader, a man who always searched beyond his immediate occupation for some way to make his presence felt. It was never in the cards that he would give up a habit of 60 years.[24]

Another fascinating president was Theodore Roosevelt, of whom I wrote earlier. Years before he succeeded William McKinley in the White House, Roosevelt was in Washington as the assistant secretary of the navy. In that role, he quickly became recognized as one of the best informed and most influential men in Washington. The *Boston Sunday Globe* applauded him as by far the most entertaining performer in "the great theater of our national life." But then the paper warned, "It would never do . . . to permit such a man to get into the presidency. He would produce national insomnia."

Moses—God's Chosen Leader

As you can guess, I've been observing presidents for a lifetime and I've never been bored. This hobby has served me well in assessing other religious and political leaders. In this chapter, I'm drawing on those years of observation in analyzing what accounts for Moses' greatness. How did he get into the leadership role? The obvious answer, of course, is the same as the answer to the scared Israelite's question: "Who made you ruler and judge over us?" God did. The answer wasn't obvious then, though. God still had a lot of sculpting to do on His chosen servant. But He would do it. We shall see that this chapter, like all the chapters in this book, is not just about the people who populate its pages. It's about God who acts through His chosen leaders. More specifically in this case, it's about what God got when He chose Moses.

Chosen for His Decisiveness

Harry Truman summarized the lot of a leader when he placed on his White House desk those famous words, "The Buck Stops Here." Others may equivocate, vacillate, and procrastinate, but a leader has to decide and take the consequences. Thus Moses. He saw a wrong and righted it. He brought justice to the abused Israelite. Unfortunately, he saw one wrong and committed another one. He saved an Israelite but killed an Egyptian.

He took decisive action, but the quick action that solved one problem only caused a much larger one.

His was the plight of all decisive people. They can decide, but they aren't always right. (Of most such persons it is often said, "Oh, he's not always right, but he's never unsure.") Timid bystanders who fail to act on their convictions are not bashful to point out that decisive people are sometimes, perhaps even often, wrong. Thank God they, the cautious ones, don't make so many mistakes. But then they don't make much of anything else, for that matter. They wait, watch, temporize, and criticize. God doesn't need any more critics. He needs decision makers.

And God doesn't require perfection. "All have sinned and fall short of the glory of God" was written of deciders and hesitators alike. When you look over the list of God's chosen leaders, you can name many who were decisive. You can't name one who was perfect. The Bible takes an unblinking view of humanity. It does not cover up Moses' temper, Noah's drunkenness, Jacob's lying, David's lust, or Peter's impetuosity. In spite of their shortcomings, God used them—in part because they could decide.

I suspect God was sympathetic with Abraham Lincoln's defense of Ulysses S. Grant during the Civil War. The president was badgered throughout General Grant's service to him with demands that he be fired. Grant's critics accused him of drunkenness, of insensitivity and even brutality toward the men who served under him, and of incompetence and mismanagement in battle. In a well-known near-midnight conversation with the president's friend A.K. McClure, McClure said he spoke for many Republicans in demanding Grant's ouster. He and Lincoln talked for two hours. The president responded with a long silence, then finally said, "I can't spare this man—he fights."

I can imagine God listening to the arguments against this Israelite-turned-Egyptian-turned-murderer-turned-refugee, then silently appraising the mistaken, impulsive, fear-driven shepherd and concluding, "I can't spare this man. He fights."

He's decisive.

Chosen for His Strength

The text doesn't tell us exactly how he killed the Egyptian. I may be reading too much into the story, but I can't help feeling that Moses was physically imposing. I can't imagine someone of my build and muscularity (or lack thereof) overpowering and slaying an Egyptian official. Probably my reading is colored by articles I've read in my president-watching years about the sheer energy that is required to run for the presidency and

then successfully measure up to its demands. Knowing what
we know of Moses' later career in the exhausting years in the
wilderness also makes it easy to believe that he was a person of
extraordinary strength.

Not just physical strength, either. Acts 7:22 tells us that
"Moses was educated in all the wisdom of the Egyptians and
was powerful in speech and action." Physical might and men-
tal power met in the man. Beyond doubt, this was someone
accustomed to winning battles both intellectual and physical.
He took on the brutal taskmaster without a doubt that he
would win.

His flaw was his temper, no doubt. But in time God would
temper his temper and redirect his strength. Moses would learn
that spiritual strength is not to be confused with machismo.
The task ahead for Moses could not be accomplished by his
abilities alone. If God called him, God would provide the
power. God would also redefine leadership as a heightened
form of service, not mere dominance. On his own, Moses could
rescue one man. To save a nation, on the other hand, would
require the cooperation of other strong leaders and the inner
resources only God could supply.

A modern parallel can be drawn between God's preparation
of Moses for leading Israel to freedom and the wilderness years
of Winston Churchill, England's great World War II leader. As a
young man, Churchill was both physically and mentally
strong. He, too, was the object of his countrymen's scorn; he
was a would-be leader whom nobody was following. Few listened as he repeatedly warned against the growing menace of
Hitler's Nazism on the continent. If many believed, they were
silent. So Churchill could do nothing but brood and bide his
time. When Europe fell to Hitler, though, England summoned
Churchill to leadership, and he responded with strong, decisive
command. Years later, he nobly gave the credit for the victory
to his fellow countrymen. "It was the nation and the race
dwelling around the globe that had the lion's heart. I had the
luck to be called upon to give the roar," he said. As far as

Churchill was concerned, he had finally realized his great leadership potential in his alliance with his people.

World War II produced many leaders and many different lessons in leadership. There were greats and near-greats among the men who commanded the various armies. The U.S. General George S. Patton was one of the near-greats who never made it all the way to the top. He was decisive. He was strong. As General Omar Bradley observed, however, he was successful as a corps commander but could climb no higher, since he never really learned to command himself. Today, Patton is remembered more for his famous profanity, growled in a profusion of often quite original expletives, than for his successes in battle. He could not be trusted with top command, Bradley believed, because he had never reined himself in.[25]

It's a lesson Moses learned well. When later we see him badgered by the exasperating pettiness of his people with their everlasting demands, we marvel at his patience, at his petitioning God again and again on their behalf. Even in the depths of his own personal discouragement, he does not give up on them or storm from his post in disgust. He exhibits perhaps the greatest strength of all—the tenacity to keep on when the opposition seems nearly overpowering.

Chosen for His Sense of Justice

It is this third quality, his sense of justice, that separates Moses most certainly from the near-greats. His decisiveness alone could have led him nowhere. Lots of street brawlers can make decisions and act quickly. They are quick to decide, quick to fight, quick to kill. Moses' strength by itself could be like that of muscle-bound weightlifters who have power that is for show only; or of some intellectual heavyweights we could mention, full of sound and fury and signifying nothing.

But Moses' sense of justice is the quality that eventually defined his life's purpose. He was offended that his fellow Hebrews were being treated like beasts of burden. He would come to their rescue.

Leaders think beyond themselves. They are ready to sacrifice their comfort, their safety, even their lives, if necessary, for others. This is why we revere Jesus as the greatest leader of all. He had the most to give up, and He gave it. He asked nothing for himself. He wanted people treated right. More than that, He wanted them to enjoy an eternity with each other and with God. He knew that only He could make that possible, so He did what only He could.

Rare are those persons who, when emotions are running high, will jump into the arena on behalf of the oppressed. Even rarer are those who move beyond mere justice to mercy. "Father, forgive them," Jesus' words from the cross on behalf of His persecutors, still cause us to marvel.

May I quote Churchill again? He expressed amazement at the gallantry of General Grant at Appomattox on April 9, 1865, the end of the American Civil War. The overpowered South had surrendered. The Union army was victorious. Victorious, but not vindictive. The head of the Confederate army, General Robert E. Lee, explained to General Grant that his officers owned their own horses. He requested they be allowed to keep them. Grant could have said they did not deserve this favor, since they had used those horses in battle against Grant's forces. Instead of taking his revenge, though, Grant replied, "Have all of them take their horses, the enlisted men and the officers as well; they will need them to plow their fields." Churchill called this one of the war's greatest moments. "In the squalor of life and war, what a magnificent act."[26]

Young Moses had not yet reached the level of General Grant's mercy at Appomattox. He certainly had much to learn before reaching Jesus' standard of mercy on the cross. But in rescuing his abused fellow Hebrew, his indignation in the face of gross injustice compelled him to act. This is the stuff leaders are made of. He had nothing to gain for himself and much to lose, yet he acted. Unlike many leader wannabes, he did not act in order to become somebody but in order to help.

Chosen for His Separation From His People

"It's lonely at the top." If it is possible to be a genuine leader and not experience loneliness, I don't know how it's done. Everything I have studied about the great leaders leads to the same conclusion. It really *is* lonely at the top. Moses' flight to Midian, his solitary years tending sheep, and his isolation from his Egyptian connections and Hebrew kinfolk seem to be essential preparation for later leadership. Think of David in flight from the mad King Saul, Jesus' forty days of temptation in the wilderness, and Paul's post-Damascus years isolated from his new Christian brothers and sisters before Barnabas brought him into church leadership. Reflect on Nelson Mandela's twenty-eight years in prison, Churchill's years in political exile, Charles de Gaulle's banishment from France's government, and Jawaharlal Nehru's imprisonment for resistance to England's colonial government before becoming India's first prime minister.

To a lesser degree, heads of most nongovernmental organizations, religious and secular, also experience some form of social ostracism. Because their every action is watched, their every word weighed, their every misstep broadcasted, they can have few if any friends and, within the organization, no peers.

And like Moses, they usually suffer the ingratitude of their people. "Who made you ruler and judge over us?" Later, time and again, the people would turn against Moses. They'd even beg to return to Egypt and to bondage, preferring slavery under Pharaoh to Moses' uncertain generalship. Even his top lieutenants, including his brother Aaron and sister Miriam, would desert him. No one would fully understand. They would not completely trust him.

Let's think about this for a moment. If you are the typical reader of this book, you are involved in your church, active in some ministry, and probably in some leadership role. If you have been at it long, you've already experienced this sense of separation. You have been let down. People have not been dependable. You know what it is like to feel used and abused.

Your labor has not been appreciated. It often seems your love for your fellow Christians has not been returned.

A large church pastor once lamented that the larger his church became, the more he was forced into loneliness. While he regretted his isolation, he found it wasn't all bad. The good that came of this by-product of success, he discovered, was that he had to turn to Christ in a more intentional way. He could not lean on anybody else's spirituality. He was on his own before the Lord.

I have thought long and hard on this subject. I'm a social being. I derive joy from the company of others. I am dependent, perhaps too dependent, on my friends and loved ones. Their opinions matter to me; I want them to like me. Unfortunately, my desire to please them makes me more susceptible to their influence than I ought to be. Compromise comes too quickly; I instinctively seek the peaceful solution, doing my best to make everybody happy and avoid conflict.

And yet I can't keep them all happy. To please some is to disappoint others. Since my job is a public one, I have had to accept the fact that at no time will everybody be happy with me, and I have probably managed at one time or another to disappoint everybody. What am I to do?

What I recommend that you do. Seek to serve the Lord and please Him in all things. Let Him be your guide, your companion, your solace. He's good company. His Word is "a lamp unto your feet." His Spirit is with you always. Let your ultimate dependency be on Him, not on family or friends or countrymen. Let Him be the one critic whose judgment you value above all others. You'll find He's easier to satisfy than the rest of your critics. He's more objective, and a lot more merciful.

Chosen for His Subordination to God

Moses' dependency on God accounts for his leadership effectiveness more than any other factor we have looked at. This is not mentioned in the verses that inform this chapter, but look carefully at Exodus 2:12. Moses decided to take things into his own hands: "Glancing this way and that and seeing no one, he killed the Egyptian and hid him in the sand."

Now put that together with verses 24 and 25: "God heard their groaning and he remembered his covenant with Abraham, with Isaac and with Jacob. So God looked on the Israelites and was concerned about them."

The contrast between these verses reminds us again that the passages we are studying in this book, while we are focusing on the struggles of Jacob, Joseph, and Moses, are themselves more concerned with God. The movement is Godward—from self-directed to God-directed lives. While Moses was taking things into his own hands he was unaware that things were already in God's hands. Moses tackled the immediate problem and paid for the unintended consequences. God was at the same time making plans for Israel, plans that included Moses. The young Moses would not do. An older, wiser man was required for the job God had in mind. Moses needed tempering. He required solitude. He would have to be captured by a greater vision.

Not a bad reminder for you and me, is it? While we have been wrestling with our own demons, trying to make a difference in our own little circles of influence, do you suppose God has been making plans for us as well? One of my strongest convictions is that God doesn't waste anything in our lives if we give ourselves to Him. I'm not being original, of course. I'm just echoing Romans 8:28—"And we know that in all things God works for the good of those who love him, who have been called according to his purpose." If you agree with Paul here, and if you love God and are obedient to Him, you have already experienced how much better it is to subordinate yourself to God's will than impose your own. What does this obedience to God mean for you, then? A little reflection is in order:

- You may have done some impulsive things—like Moses.
- You may have committed some really terrible crime—like Moses.

- You may have spent many years of your life in seemingly boring, unchallenging routines—like Moses.
- You may not have been called into any leadership role yet—like Moses, who didn't become a leader until he was eighty.
- You may have a growing desire to bring about justice or a forming sense of purpose in your life—like Moses.
- You may be developing some useful, positive characteristics—like Moses, who didn't reach full capacity until taking on a job that required everything he had to give.

If so, then don't be surprised when God calls you to a new ministry, a new sphere of service, a new responsibility that He has been preparing you for. If you let God use you, then like Moses you may find yourself a leader in spite of yourself—if not of a nation like Israel, then in your community, your church, your occupation, your neighborhood, or your family. Israel was in desperate need of someone to lead the nation to freedom. God provided Moses.

God Prepares Us to Lead

Many centuries later, the newly forming Christian church was also in need. A missionary was required to carry the Gospel from the Jews to the Gentiles, a daunting task demanding extraordinary skill. God filled the bill with Saul of Tarsus, the man we know better as the apostle Paul. The impact of this former persecutor of Christians was so profound that some scholars have even erroneously called him the real founder of Christianity. Paul would one day assure his friends in Philippi, "My God will meet all your needs according to his glorious riches in Christ Jesus" (Philippians 4:19). He had certainly met all of Paul's. I can't read this verse without a smile. Paul was writing about the future, but in truth, God had already met some of the Philippians' most urgent needs. The greatest gift He gave them was none other than Paul himself.

Which leads to this last sobering question: Is it possible that God has been preparing you as His gift to somebody? Your church? Your neighborhood? Your circle of acquaintances? Your nation? God gave the Israelites Moses. He gave the Philippians Paul. He gave the world Jesus. And He has given you to . . . ?

You will recognize that I'm drawing from Ephesians 4:11-13 here. In this letter, Paul asserts that God "gave some to be apostles, some to be prophets, some to be evangelists, and some to be pastors and teachers, to prepare God's people for works of service, so that the body of Christ may be built up until we all reach unity in the faith and in the knowledge of the Son of God and become mature, attaining to the whole measure of the fullness of Christ." His subject is the church, but what strikes us is that in Paul's view, God is responsible for outfitting the church with the people that the church needs to do its job. Some are in leadership roles (apostles, prophets, evangelists, pastors, and teachers) and the rest in servant roles ("people for works of service"), but they are all gifts of God for the church.

I like thinking of you and me as gifts of God, don't you? Especially since we have Paul's assurance that "my God will meet all your needs according to his glorious riches in Christ Jesus" (Philippians 4:19).

The only remaining question is what (or whom) we are good for? As I said, we may never become a nation builder like Moses or a church builder like Paul, but like Jesus, we can become God's instrument for rescuing the world—at least our section of it. Through us God can take care of some of the people who need Him.

A pretty exciting thought, don't you agree?

6

How God Calls
a Leader

Exodus 3:1-22

Moses' wilderness period, as we saw in the last chapter, was essential preparation for leadership greatness. It was in Midian that his faith deepened, his convictions were firmed up, and his insights into himself and his God clarified. I called attention to the similarity between Moses and Jesus, whose forty days in the wilderness parallel Moses' experience. I also mentioned some of our more recent political leaders. Like Moses, these were old men when called to serve their countries. Winston Churchill, for example, was sixty-six when called to his wartime office. He finally stepped down as prime minister the last time when he was eighty. Charles de Gaulle had to wait until he was sixty-seven to create France's Fifth Republic, which he then led until he was seventy-eight. Germans called their leader, Konrad Adenauer, *Der Alte*, the Old Man, because he was seventy-three when he took the reins as chancellor and remained in office until he was eighty-seven. For each of these men and many others, it was first the wilderness, then the call.

For anyone aspiring to leadership in God's kingdom, a closer look at Moses' call pays dividends. While we may never be asked to lead a nation, as we noted earlier, God's dealings with Moses have much to teach us—wherever He calls us to serve.

God Comes in an Awe-Inspiring Vision

> Now Moses was tending the flock of Jethro his father-in-law, the priest of Midian, and he led the flock to the far side of the desert and came to Horeb, the mountain of God. There the angel of the LORD appeared to him in flames of fire from within a bush. Moses saw that though the bush was on fire it did not burn up. So Moses thought, "I will go over and see this strange sight—why the bush does not burn up" (Exodus 3:1-3).

Whether it is a seminar on organizational management or a class in personal leadership, the opening lesson is always the same: First comes the vision. The vision defines purpose. It stimulates action and gives direction. It energizes. For decades, this powerhouse of a man had been quietly tending sheep, apparently content riding the rhythm of the seasons, caught in the unchallenging routines of sheep tending. He would have died as he lived, unnoticed, unsought, and unproductive (at least as measured by his potential) except that one special day, he saw a burning bush and heard a voice he knew was God's.

> When the LORD saw that he had gone over to look, God called to him from within the bush, "Moses! Moses!"
> And Moses said, "Here I am."
> "Do not come any closer," God said. "Take off your sandals, for the place where you are standing is holy ground." Then he said, "I am the God of your father, the God of Abraham, the God of Isaac and the God of Jacob." At this, Moses hid his face, because he was afraid to look at God (Exodus 3:4-6).

A vision and a voice. One minute a sheepherder, the next the shepherd of a vast multitude of people. Before, a refugee from

Pharaoh. After, a challenger of and eventual champion over Pharaoh. It began—it always begins—with a vision.

A Church With a Vision

When I retired as pastor of Central Christian Church, the congregation's weekend attendance averaged around 4,500. When I was called to become the church's leader twenty years earlier, the attendance averaged 490. As you can imagine, the intervening years were quite a ride, one that meant selling our property and relocating, camping for nineteen months in the local high school auditorium while the new building was under construction, incurring and nearly drowning in a humongous debt, struggling to attain financial stability, building more buildings, establishing another congregation, developing an exciting worldwide missions program, and on and on.

I wish I could tell you that I was the reason for this progress. I wasn't. I'm not even the one who saw the burning bush. It had been spotted before my family and I moved from Indiana to Arizona.

The elders told me about the sighting during the job interview. They had seen a vision of a large, flagship church in the East Valley of Greater Phoenix. They believed their congregation should be that church. They wanted us to move from Indianapolis, they said, because I was serving a larger congregation there and would know how to help them bring the vision to reality. Their consecrated vision inspired us, so we moved.

Later, that same congregation demonstrated that it could "see" another's vision and make it their own. This happened in 1990, eleven years after our move to Mesa. Pacific Christian College, which later became Hope International University, needed a new president. Dr. Knofel Staton, who had served the school well, was forced out of office by deteriorating health. His heart was failing him. Because of my earlier academic career at Milligan College in Tennessee, the trustees of PCC

asked me to move to Fullerton and assume the presidency. I
couldn't, I told them. It would be unethical for this pastor to
leave Central at that stage "because I have them so far in debt,"
I explained. After awhile, the trustees returned with another
proposition: All right, they said, don't leave, but come anyway.

They believed it would serve the best interests of the college
to have a president who was modeling the institution's values.
PCC was preparing ministers for full-time Christian service.
Let the president lead the way. It was a bold vision, not exactly
unprecedented but not endorsed either by the accrediting association that insists that accredited colleges and universities
must be led by presidents who give full time to their office.

Perhaps you can imagine my nervousness when I presented
PCC's invitation to our staff and eldership at Central. In fact, I
was so nervous, I didn't present it. Four trustees came to Mesa
to meet with the church's leadership team. I let them make the
pitch.

I could hardly believe the result. All four bodies—the
church's elders and staff, and the college's faculty and
trustees—voted unanimously to follow the vision. (And later,
the accreditation association approved the exception to their
guidelines.) From the church's perspective, and this is the reason I'm telling the story, it was just another example of faithfulness to their original vision. They wanted to be the East
Valley's flagship church. They had made it clear to me in that
initial interview that they wanted to serve not only Mesa, or
the East Valley, or Arizona, or even the United States, but the
world. They saw my work at Pacific Christian College as a logical extension of their own congregational commitment to missions. It was, if you please, more of the same.

The "unique partnership," as the chairman of the elders
dubbed the new relationship between the church and college,
blessed both bodies. The church continued to grow in numbers
and mission impact, and the college was reinvigorated when
this major church "adopted" it in this bold way. My dual role
lasted for nine years, until Cal Jernigan, my able successor,

stepped into the senior minister's position at the church.

The point of this excursion into autobiography is to assure you that I'm a believer in the importance of vision and have often (as in these two instances) benefited from someone else's. I can't claim always to have seen the burning bush myself, but I can join forces with those who have.

Called Through a Vision

The experiences of Moses and Isaiah stand as two of the most dramatic instances of God's calling through vision.

> In the year that King Uzziah died, I saw the Lord seated on a throne, high and exalted, and the train of his robe filled the temple. Above him were seraphs, each with six wings: With two wings they covered their faces, with two they covered their feet, and with two they were flying. And they were calling to one another:
> "Holy, holy, holy is the LORD Almighty; the whole earth is full of his glory."
> At the sound of their voices the doorposts and thresholds shook and the temple was filled with smoke.
> "Woe to me!" I cried. "I am ruined! For I am a man of unclean lips, and I live among a people of unclean lips, and my eyes have seen the King, the LORD Almighty."
> Then one of the seraphs flew to me with a live coal in his hand, which he had taken with tongs from the altar. With it he touched my mouth and said, "See, this has touched your lips; your guilt is taken away and your sin atoned for."
> Then I heard the voice of the Lord saying, "Whom shall I send? And who will go for us?"
> And I said, "Here am I. Send me!" (Isaiah 6:1-8)

Like Moses, Isaiah was overwhelmed by a sense of God's holiness and of his own unworthiness to be in the presence of God. The temple, like the area around the bush, had become "holy ground." Not a place for "a man of unclean lips" who lived "among a people of unclean lips."

It's the same experience Job went through. His encounter
with God came less abruptly, though. He had already lost
everything—his family, his wealth, his health, and even, thanks
to his well-intentioned but nonetheless maddening friends, his
peace of mind—when the Lord spoke to him in the midst of a
fierce storm. It wasn't a pleasant encounter. God asked him a
whole series of questions to put him in his place (see Job 38).
Finally, it was Job's turn. He sounds like Isaiah and Moses:

> My ears had heard of you
> But now my eyes have seen you.
> Therefore I despise myself
> And repent in dust and ashes (Job 42:5, 6).

It seems inevitable, doesn't it, that a vision of God should
lead to self-reproach. Who am I that I should presume to serve
this holy God?

Several of my fellow pastors have experienced the kind of
growth in their churches that was ours in Mesa. When we get
together to compare notes, you hear very little boasting.
Instead, you hear wonderment, even astonishment. And the
similar thread running through all of our comments is, "Who
am I . . . ?" There's nothing ritualistic about our praise: "To God
be the glory, great things HE has done."

Both Moses and Isaiah grasped God's purpose in appearing
before them. Isaiah got the point quickly: "Whom shall I send?
And who will go for us?" God asked. Isaiah answered, "Here
am I. Send me!"

With Moses it took longer, as we shall see below. But it took.

The Stewards of Vision

Today's leading management guru Peter Drucker's often-
quoted observation comes to mind here. "Whenever anything
is being accomplished, it is being done, I have learned, by a
monomaniac with a mission."[27] But where does this single-
minded passion come from? It originates in the vision that

inspires it. Robert Menzies of Australia once commented that Churchill (who keeps appearing on these pages as both a student and an example of leadership) delivered such stirring messages because he himself had learned the great truth "that to move other people, the speaker, the leader, must first move himself." Whether moved by the bush, or the temple seraphim and the voice of God, or a vision of a flagship church in the East Valley, or whatever vision God gives you—as a leader you are the steward of that vision, holding it high before your people, speaking of it, describing it, explaining it, incarnating it while urging your followers to accomplish it.

So for the next forty years of his life, Moses would keep returning to the God who spoke in the burning bush. What do you want me to do? What is right for these people? What is the next step? What are our values? What would you have this liberated nation become? How can I most faithfully fulfill the vision?

God Makes Fearful Demands

> I have indeed seen the misery of my people in Egypt. I have heard them crying out because of their slave drivers, and I am concerned about their suffering (Exodus 3:7).

God opened His heart to Moses. In that moment, God's concern became Moses' concern. When you've heard the voice of God, you can never again foist the problem off onto someone else, asking, as so many do, "Why don't *they* do something?" The *they* has become *we* or, even more frighteningly, *I*.

Moses' response was immediate, automatic, and completely human: "Who, me?" "Who am I?" Listen in on this conversation.

> "So now, go. I am sending you to Pharaoh to bring my people the Israelites out of Egypt."
> . . . "Who am I, that I should go . . . ?"

. . . "I will be with you. . . ."

. . . "Suppose I go to the Israelites and say to them, 'The God of your fathers has sent me to you,' and they ask me, 'What is his name?' Then what shall I tell them?"

"I AM WHO I AM. This is what you are to say to the Israelites: 'I AM has sent me to you'" (Exodus 3:10-14).

For Moses, this was a doubly awesome encounter. He was awed by the presence of God, no doubt. But he was in awe, as well, of the magnitude of the assignment God was giving him. "Who, me? Against Pharaoh? With my stumbling tongue? With my checkered history? Oh, please, God, not me."

Everything in Moses wanted to say *no*, but God says *yes*.

My first assistant as a very young minister was a man in his mid-sixties. Rynie Karls had been forced to retire as a fireman because his smoke-damaged lungs made it impossible to continue. The fire department's loss was Tigard Christian Church's gain. Rynie kept our building in spotless condition. He also helped me with pastoral calling. He was a wise counselor, cherished friend, and deeply loved leader in the church. Many years after I had moved away from Oregon, Rynie told me, "You taught me I could do things I never thought I could do. You made me believe in myself." I appreciated the compliment but I didn't have it coming. What happened in our relationship was simply this: His desires were my desires. We just teamed up. It never dawned on me that he couldn't do the tasks I gave him and he never told me he couldn't do them. We both were captured by a vision of what God wanted that little church in Tigard to become, so we worked side by side to make the vision concrete. He was a little timid. I was really scared, an inexperienced twenty-one-year-old planting a church. I was convinced that only God could pull it off, and He did.

Leadership Takes Courage

Richard Nixon, driven from the White House in disgrace, spent his retirement years rebuilding his reputation. He wrote some excellent books, including *Leaders*, in which he muses on the qualities that make a leader a leader. Here is one of his lists: intelligence, instinct, character, belief in a cause. To this catalog he adds, "But many have these qualities; very few have the indispensable quality for political success—to risk all to gain all. You must not be afraid to lose. This does not mean you should be rash. But above all you must be bold."[28] He sounds somewhat like the apostle Paul, doesn't he?

> But whatever was to my profit I now consider loss for the sake of Christ.
> What is more, I consider everything a loss compared to the surpassing greatness of knowing Christ Jesus my Lord, for whose sake I have lost all things. I consider them rubbish, that I may gain Christ. . . . Brothers, I do not consider myself yet to have taken hold of it. But one thing I do: Forgetting what is behind and straining toward what is ahead, I press on toward the goal to win the prize for which God has called me heavenward in Christ Jesus (Philippians 3:7, 8, 13, 14).

During the years of strenuous growth at Central Christian and as we were debating whether or not to take on yet another major building project, Dr. Jess Conant, one of our elders, warned us, "We're being too timid." I long remembered his words because they are not typical of church leaders (they were, however, of Central's leaders). It's one thing to see the vision; it's quite another to find the courage to follow it.

Machiavelli's *The Prince*—written to advise aspiring kings how to grasp and hold power—is probably a strange source to be quoting in a book on biblical leadership. Machiavelli, however, reached the same conclusion from a very secular perspective: "There is nothing more difficult to carry out, nor more doubtful of success, nor more dangerous to handle, than to initiate a new order of things."

The messiness of change—that's what bogs us down. The complications, the politics, the sheer hard work, and the fearful exhaustion of the daily grind—these threaten to overwhelm us. We marvel at the purity of the vision; we cower before the frightening power plays, frustrations, defeats, delays, and multitudinous details to be attended to. There's so much risk.

Leadership Takes Risks

In the last century, no one wrote more loftily of spiritual things than the great Russian author Count Leo Tolstoy. He so badly wanted to be a saint. He devoted himself to pursuing a vision of personal holiness. Yet this man who wrote so loftily about burning bushes found family life almost unbearable. The noise, the confusion, the tensions of interpersonal relations under one roof drove him from the family several times. Finally, he left for good. Away from them, he wrote, lived like a peasant, and boasted that he thought "no more of man, but only of God." He may have thought so, but his old servant Agatha Mikhailovna wasn't fooled. She shook her head at Tolstoy and grumbled, "You've left the Countess back there to carry on alone with eight children, while you sit here pulling at your beard."[29] She was not impressed.

God won't allow it, this self-centered beard pulling. He won't let Moses content himself with writing his memoirs of his experience with God at the burning bush. He has work to do. He can't merely feel sorry for his enslaved fellow Hebrews. He must rescue them. It's a frightening job, but somebody has to do it. And he's the somebody.

Over the years, I've gained a lot help from E. Stanley Jones, whose ministry in India gave him valuable insight into the mind of God. Once, when he went to the Garden of Gethsemane in the Holy Land to spend the night in prayer, he planned to center his meditation on what he thought was the heart and substance of the Gethsemane incident—Jesus' final renunciation of His own desires in favor of God's: "Not my will, but yours be done." Dr. Jones said he expected to come away feeling chastened, submissive, surrendered.

But he said that instead, in those silent hours, he found his thoughts "shifting to the words of Jesus to the sleepy disciples, 'Arise, let us be going'—to meet the betrayal, the rejection, the accusations, the spittle, the cross. The will of God was to be done, not by acquiescence but by activity." Not the feeling of spirituality, but actions that are spiritually motivated—these are what the Lord calls for.

"I came away from Gethsemane," he concluded, "not depressed into submission, as I thought I would be, but with a battle cry sounding in my heart. Gethsemane meant to me no longer a sigh and a tear and a submission, but the call to arise and be going to meet everything, even in the very worst that can happen to us, and to turn it into a testimony of the love of God."[30]

What Dr. Jones experienced at Gethsemane seems to me to be the goal of genuine worship of God, whether before a burning bush or in a seraph-inhabited temple or in a contemporary worship center with the praise band and worship team carrying enthusiastic worshipers to glory. The purpose is not to entertain or soothe or even chastise the congregation. These are good results, to be sure. But the purpose is to recharge, refuel, and ready the people to get on with their work for God.

I don't know whether Nikos Kazantzakis is right or not, but I suspect he is. In his novel *St. Francis*, he depicts Francis talking to his disciple and companion.

> "Brother Leo," he tells him, "the only joy in this world is to do God's will. Do you know why?"
> "How should I know, Brother Francis? Enlighten me."
> "Because what God wants, that, and only that, is also what we want—but we don't know it. God comes and awakens our souls, revealing to them their real, though unknown, desire. This is the secret, Brother Leo. To do the will of God means to do my own most deeply hidden will. Within even the most unworthy of men there is a servant of God, asleep."[31]

If St. Francis is right, God called Moses to do what he wanted to do forty years earlier, but couldn't. He was upset then by the injustice of Egyptian tyranny. He could rescue one Hebrew; he could not save the nation. But then God met Moses in the deepest concerns of his heart, out in the wilderness, where he was undoubtedly still brooding over Egypt's brutality. And God said in effect, "Now you go and do what you, as well as I, believe should be done."

A frightening commission. A completely appropriate one, if indeed Moses wanted to see his people liberated.

God Promises His Abiding Presence

With God, commission always means companionship. He does not send His chosen ones to do battle alone. "Surely, I am with you always," Jesus promised, "to the very end of the age" (Matthew 28:20). "The Lord is my shepherd, I shall not be in want. . . . Your rod and your staff, they comfort me," David sang in Psalm 23. He had personally experienced God's companionship. "The LORD is my light and my salvation—whom shall I fear? The LORD is the stronghold of my life—of whom shall I be afraid?" (Psalm 27:1).

Later, when he had the people safely across the Red Sea, Moses and the people sang a new song:

> I will sing to the LORD, for he is highly exalted.
> The horse and its rider he has hurled into the sea.
> The LORD is my strength and my song; he has become my
>   salvation.
> He is my God, and I will praise him, my father's God, and
>   I will exalt him (Exodus 15:1, 2).

Even God's name was a source of reassurance to the doubting Moses. Earlier Moses protested, "Who am I? Why did You give me this assignment, God? You know my shortcomings, my inadequacies. Just who do You think I am?"

That's an important question, all right. But then Moses asked an even more important one: "Who are You?" It's bigger than it sounds. "Who are You that I should trust You? Who are You that I should leave Your territory, the realm in which I know You to be sovereign, to go to Egypt where other gods hold sway, where Your ways and Your people seem weak and ineffectual. Who are You *there*, God?"

"I AM who I AM." I am not *a* god among other gods. My name is not *a* name over against other names. My name does not limit or define me nor does geography fence me in. I am unlimited, undefined, indescribable, beyond imagining. But I AM. And I am who I am without reference to any other being or place or power. I am beyond the limitations of vocabulary and I dwell within and beyond the borders of any territory. I am known by my actions. You know that I was with your ancestors Abraham, Isaac, and Jacob. Now I will be to you what I was to them and I will be with you as I was with them. You can count on me. Trust me. "I AM who I AM."

As he was obedient to this burning-bush vision, Moses would learn what the famed missionary J. Hudson Taylor also discovered many centuries later: "God's work, done in God's way, will never lack God's supply."

It's a truth Moses can count on.

So can we.

7

Did God Choose the Wrong Person?

Exodus 4:1-23

In preparing most of the chapters in this book, I have had to read other writers for deeper insight into the themes we are exploring. Not so with this one. On this subject, I am qualified to write. The subject is doubt. Not the kind of doubt that unsettles faith, nor the healthy kind that paves the way for learning, but self-doubt—the often crippling lack of confidence in one's ability to succeed. Doubt that makes excuses, doubt that hides from responsibility, doubt that leads to what one of my friends calls "intellectual paralysis" (the inability to make a decision out of fear of being wrong). My kind of doubt.

When I was younger, I thought that as we grew older and more experienced, self-confidence would just naturally increase. Wrong. There's a reason why older people joke about how much they used to know, how they could lick the world when they were twenty but in their sixties it's a struggle just to survive. I can hardly believe what has happened to me, how hesitant I have become, how unsure of myself. And with age has come this irritating ability, one I never sought, to see both sides of an issue. Many of my blacks and whites have blended into grays. Once I could have aspired to political leadership, fantasizing about the governor's mansion or maybe a senate seat (the White House, even to my unbridled imagination, was out of reach). Today I marvel that anyone would want the jobs and I would run, not walk, from any hint that I should aspire to them. I'm not up to the task. Boy, do I understand Moses' reluctance to serve. I would turn God down, too.

Where is the brash young Moses, so fearless in defending his fellow Hebrew, so quick to dispense justice with his bare hands? What have his years in the wilderness done to him? He has aged another forty years, of course. And he has added more, much more wisdom, no doubt, but certainly not more self-confidence. To the contrary. This is one man who's definitely not running for office. So when God asked Moses to lead the Israelites out of Egypt, Moses had plenty of excuses why he was not the man for the job.

Moses' Excuse: They Might Not Believe Me

What if he were to do as God asked him? Who would believe the man? And why should they? If they knew anything of his past, this pampered son of the palace, this hotheaded judge and executioner, what would cause them to trust him now?

He would have to prove himself to the Israelites and Egyptians alike. Forty years earlier, he had killed an Egyptian and gone AWOL, never to return. Not exactly the best credentials for negotiating with the king. Forty years earlier, he had deserted the Hebrews, abandoning his own people to their fate. Why would they want to follow someone like him? When he turns up, decades later, and announces, "From now on I am your leader. You must follow me," why should they? Can you imagine yourself, in those circumstances, casting your lot with someone like Moses?

Even a man at the height of his powers and suffering no lack of confidence in those powers would be loathe to take on this task, wouldn't he?

God's Reply: I'll Help You Convince Them

God understood Moses' reluctance. His counterargument began:

> "What is that in your hand?"
> "A staff," he replied.
> The LORD said, "Throw it on the ground."
> Moses threw it on the ground and it became a snake, and he ran from it. Then the LORD said to him, "Reach out your hand and take it by the tail." So Moses reached out and took hold of the snake and it turned back into a staff in his hand (Exodus 4:2-4).

Grab the snake, Moses. Take hold of your fears. Do you see what you can do, Moses, when I am with you? You can tame snakes.

It's a principle of elementary psychology. If you want to overcome your fear, do something. Action feeds confidence. Inaction feeds and magnifies fear. To fight fear, act. To increase fear, don't just do something, stand there. Procrastinate, postpone, make excuses.

Two fairly recent personal experiences come to mind. I think I've told the stories of each experience in earlier books, so I won't go into great detail. Just let me tell you that when I was fifty-five, I bungee jumped 143 feet from a bridge over a river in New Zealand. Then five years later, my son-in-law and an adopted son took me skydiving as my sixtieth birthday present. My wife Joy went along as official photographer for the event. On both of those occasions, I experienced what a paratrooper instructor once explained—that the jump itself isn't so bad. It's the waiting to jump that gets you. It didn't help in New Zealand when the young man ahead of me approached the edge of the platform, hesitated, turned back, then gathered some more courage, went once again to the edge, then turned around, then. . . . The more he vacillated, the tougher it was on him. The postponing magnified his fear. And, truth to tell, it didn't make my own jump any easier, either.

As if understanding that one miracle wouldn't be enough to convince Moses that this jump into leadership was for him, God offered some additional demonstrations.

> "Put your hand inside your cloak." So Moses put his hand into his cloak, and when he took it out, it was leprous, like snow.
>
> "Now put it back into your cloak," he said. So Moses put his hand back into his cloak, and when he took it out, it was restored, like the rest of his flesh.
>
> Then the LORD said, "If they do not believe you or pay attention to the first miraculous sign, they may believe the second. But if they do not believe these two signs or listen to you, take some water from the Nile and pour it on the dry ground. The water you take from the river will become blood on the ground" (Exodus 4:6-9).

Moses found God's argument-by-miracles persuasive enough that he shifted to another complaint. But before following him there, read verses 29-31. The people find the miracles adequate reason to believe:

> Moses and Aaron brought together all the elders of the Israelites, and Aaron told them everything the LORD had said to Moses. He also performed the signs before the people, and they believed. And when they heard that the LORD was concerned about them and had seen their misery, they bowed down and worshiped.

God was fully aware of Moses' need to prove himself—both to himself and to the people—and He provided the means to do it. Today, though, the miracles wouldn't be persuasive, would they? Think of the Afghan tribesmen fighting the avenging Americans after the September 11th attacks. The United

States's technological and military superiority overwhelmed and defeated the Taliban and its sympathizers, but it did not convert them into lovers of America. Even as the war was being waged, thoughtful Americans had to admit that a different kind of argument is needed to transform enemies into allies. Air strikes and bombings can defeat but can't convert; to make friends of enemies, to make followers of doubters, you must convince them that you'll meet their social needs, feed their hunger, and share their fate. Missionaries learned long ago that if you are serious about reaching the lost in other countries, you can't come on like an occupying army. If you would lead them to the Lord, you must live with the people, learn their language, share their discomforts, heal their sick, and help them realize their dreams. You have to earn the right to present the gospel.

Not too long ago, as Joy and I were standing in line to go to the movies, a sidewalk preacher harangued the crowd, warning of the destruction of the end times and assuring us we'd be damned unless we repented. Do I need to tell you he didn't make any converts? He hadn't earned the right.

Even more recently, we were waiting for a train in the Los Angeles railroad station when a man came into the lobby, took up his position just down the bench from us, stood up, turned outward to nobody in particular, and began reading his sermon from a book. Very few of us could hear him. It didn't matter. He just kept on preaching. I wondered whether he was going by the clock. Having been assigned to preach for so many hours in the Los Angeles railroad station, he was conscientiously doing as he had been told. After awhile, the bored passengers tuned him out. They hadn't seen any miracles. They didn't believe he was concerned about them. He hadn't earned the right to a hearing, even if they had been able to hear him.

Bertolt Brecht told the story of a European peasant trapped at home when the Nazis invaded. A storm trooper came to his cottage, dragged him outside, and told him, "From now on I am in charge. I will live in your house. You will feed me and polish my boots every day. I will be the master and you the servant. If you disagree, I will kill you. Will you submit to me?"

The farmer didn't even answer. He just went to work for the storm trooper. He fed him every day, polished his boots, did whatever he was told. This went on for many months until the Allied army came through the village and liberated it. Now it was the storm trooper's turn to be dragged out of the cottage. The soldiers hauled him off to prison. Seeing what was happening, the peasant stood proudly in front of him and, speaking directly into his face, answered, "No."[32]

There had been no conversion. He had not become a believer. He never served the paratrooper. He had just submitted to force.

Moses would be asking the people to submit to his authority. He would have to be able to persuade the Israelites, because there was no way he could, even if he wanted to, overpower them as the storm trooper did. There was no way he could, by himself, convince them to believe in him. But—and this was God's goal—with divine help he could convince them that he was the instrument of the God they already believed in. Their belief in God, and their conviction that Moses was acting for Him, would make the difference.

Moses' Excuse: I Can't Talk Good

First, Moses had to overcome his fear of rejection. God gave him the tools to do that—the staff/snake, the healthy/leprous hand, the Nile water-turned-into-blood. Then he had to deal with his fear of inadequacy. "O Lord, I have never been eloquent, neither in the past nor since you have spoken to your servant. I am slow of speech and tongue" (Exodus 4:10).

In just about every survey I have ever seen on human fears, fear of speaking before an audience and fear of speaking to strangers ranks either first or among the first. Do you remember having to stand in front of your class to recite? In the early grades, you were probably eager. As you grew older, though, you became more self-conscious. By your high school years, you would have done almost anything else than "perform" before your classmates.

And what about going into a roomful of strangers? Many churches are puzzled because they aren't growing. The members don't understand why new people don't want to join their friendly group. Ah, but the question contains the answer. They are "new" people. To new people, the friendly group is a bunch of strangers, and they just don't feel comfortable talking to strangers. For a church to grow, members have to make every effort to help the new people not feel like new people. They should never be asked to go alone into the midst of strangers. It's not enough to invite them to come; someone must pick them up and bring them as their guests. Then there is at least one other person in the room who is not a stranger to them. They won't feel quite so inadequate.

We fear rejection because we feel inadequate; we feel inadequate because we are afraid we'll be rejected. One fear feeds the other.

I am very sensitive to this issue because in spite of having a reputation for being a noisy little man, I, too, feel extremely uncomfortable in a roomful of strangers and hate going alone into any group, anywhere, in which I do not know anyone. And to have to say something before a group of persons I don't know is still a frightening experience, even though I have been a public speaker for half a century.

God's Reply: I'll Help You Speak

Moses' complaint, then, seems pretty reasonable to me. Still, God's answer seems to have an edge to it: "Who gave man his mouth? Who makes him deaf or mute? Who gives him sight or makes him blind? Is it not I, the LORD? Now go; I will help you speak and will teach you what to say" (Exodus 4:11, 12). God's perspective was obviously not the same as Moses', who was thinking only of his own ability. God, however, was consider-

ing both Moses' and His own. The one who created mouths
and speech had nothing to be afraid of. Neither, He insisted,
did the one through whom God would be speaking. What
Moses needed to understand—and what I have spent a lifetime
trying to remember—is that when God calls people to do something, He also empowers them to accomplish it. Moses was
inadequate. He couldn't "speak good." But that didn't matter
when God's doing the talking.

A long time ago, I heard of a five-year-old boy named Billy
who, after thirty minutes in bed, began crying loudly. He had
watched a science-fiction film that evening and was afraid that
the little green monsters were going to kidnap him. I admire
his father. He didn't just tell his son not to worry, that nothing
was going to get him and he should get back to sleep, which,
I'm afraid, would have been my style. Instead, he put on quite
a show for the boy. He inspected the windows to be sure they
were shut tight. He checked the closet to be certain nobody was
hiding there. He examined the space under the bed. Then he
picked up one of the boy's plastic guns and put it on a table
beside his bed. "Billy, here's a gun for you just in case." Four
minutes later, Billy was fast asleep.

That's what guns (either make-believe or real) are for—to
make people who feel inadequate feel secure. People who trust
in the Lord don't need guns. Their "adequacy" is in Him.

When facing tasks that we don't feel up to, it is good to
review some of the many comforting Scriptures that remind us
we're not alone. In spite of our insufficiencies, those whose
trust is in the Lord can accomplish far beyond what is possible
on their own. Here's a favorite of mine:

> "Not by might nor by power, but by my Spirit," says the
> Lord Almighty (Zechariah 4:6).

The psalms are also a constant source of encouragement.
Here are just a few of the many reminders that people who
trust in the Lord will be rewarded:

In God, whose word I praise,
in God I trust; I will not be afraid.
What can mortal man do to me? (56:4)

Trust in him at all times, O people;
pour out your hearts to him,
for God is our refuge. (62:8)

Those who trust in the Lord are like Mount Zion,
which cannot be shaken but endures forever. (125:1)

No verse comes to mind more often, especially when I am faced with a huge project that seems far beyond my ability, than Ephesians 3:20, 21: "Now to him who is able to do immeasurably more than all we ask or imagine, according to his power that is at work within us, to him be glory in the church and in Christ Jesus throughout all generations, for ever and ever! Amen." If this passage doesn't stiffen your backbone, what will?

Moses' Refusal: I Don't Want to Do It

"O Lord, please send someone else to do it."

This was the bottom line. Blame it on a fear of rejection, excuse it as a sense of inadequacy, the truth is, Moses just didn't want to do it. God was disturbing Moses' serenity. He was at home with his sheep, at peace with his family, comfortably distanced from Egypt.

Like the fellow who could resist anything but temptation, most of us can endure anything except discomfort. If we like it, we'll give ourselves to it with enthusiasm, whether it's playing with kids, boating at the lake, making love, reading books, working out, following sports, cultivating the vital art of doing nothing, or whatever. These things matter to us. When asked to volunteer to serve, our conscience usually won't allow us to say, "I don't want to," so we make up some excuse to get ourselves out of it.

In the course of a lifetime of overseeing employees and working with other businesses and government workers, I have heard just about every kind of excuse, most of them not very honest. I did hear of a truthful one a number of years ago in the Northwest, and it made me admit that honesty alone isn't sufficient, either. A contractor had been trying to collect an overdue bill for months. He was getting nowhere. As a last resort, he sent a tear-jerking letter to his debtor and enclosed a snapshot of his little daughter. Under the picture he wrote, "The reason I must have the money."

This time he received a prompt reply. It was a photo of a voluptuous blonde in a bathing suit. It was labeled, "The reason I can't pay!"

There's always some reason why "I can't." I agree with the Greek philosopher Epictetus, who said, "The first difference between one of the crowd and a philosopher is this: the one says, 'I am undone on account of my child, my brother, my father [or my blonde girlfriend in the bathing suit]'; but the other, if ever he be obliged to say, 'I am undone!' reflects, and adds, 'on account of myself.'"

As I said, after a lifetime of supervising employees, I think I've heard just about every kind of excuse. Most of them have one thing in common. It's the truth: "I don't want to do it." Thus Moses' plea: "O Lord, please send someone else to do it."

When my friend Bob Shannon was preaching in Largo, Florida, he related this story to his congregation, "An African minister was late to church. Mabalini explained to the congregation that he was late because his bicycle had broken down and he had to walk the eight miles to church in eighty-degree heat. He is seventy years old, his feet are deformed, and he is a leper." Then after letting this tale sink in, Bob added, "Remember him when it seems too much trouble to ride two or three miles to church in your air-conditioned car!"

I think Bob, too, had heard about all the excuses he wanted to hear.

I've never been able to forget what happened in New York

City a few decades ago. As reported in *Time* magazine, two crimes were committed in May 1964. The first was the murder of Kitty Genovese in the predawn darkness of the quiet, middle-class community of Kew Gardens. The lunatic who killed her had never seen her before. The slaying took place over a thirty-five-minute period. The killer left and returned three times to stab her again and again while Miss Genovese staggered and screamed and dragged herself along the street. The bare facts are almost more than you can take in. What makes the horrific tale even more disturbing is the police's later confirmation that at least thirty-seven neighbors, awakened by Kitty's screams, had stared out their dark windows at one time or another, but none of them called the police. They didn't want to get involved!

The same article in *Time* reported, "An eighteen-year-old switchboard [operator] named Olga Romero hurtled naked and screaming down the stairs of a building on a busy East Tremont Avenue in the Bronx. In the vestibule, in plain sight of the street (the door was open), she lay screaming and bleeding, while a man struggled to drag her upstairs again. 'Help me!' she cried again and again. 'He raped me.' Heads popped out of offices along the hallway, and a crowd of about forty gathered outside to watch. No one made any move on her behalf. No one called the police."[33]

If you have lived in a large city, you can perhaps sympathize with the New Yorkers. All kinds of complications can arise when you reach out to help someone. You could be accused, attacked, or sued. Good Samaritans run many risks. You can understand. But can you excuse?

"Help me," the women cried.

"I don't want to," the silence answered.

If you can understand the New Yorkers, you can certainly identify with Moses.

"Help my people in Egypt."

"I don't want to, Lord. Send someone else."

God's Reply: I'll Take Care of Everything—
Now Get to Work!

I would be curious how this conversation between God and
Moses is understood by people who claim that their God is so
loving, He never disapproves, never chastises, never gets
angry. It seems pretty clear to me:

> *Then the LORD's anger burned against Moses* and he said,
> "What about your brother, Aaron the Levite? I know he
> can speak well. He is already on his way to meet you, and
> his heart will be glad when he sees you. You shall speak to
> him and put words in his mouth; I will help both of you
> speak and will teach you what to do. He will speak to the
> people for you, and it will be as if he were your mouth and
> as if you were God to him. But take this staff in your hand
> so you can perform miraculous signs with it" (Exodus
> 4:14-17, italics mine).

This is the same God Jesus spoke about in the parable of the
last judgment (Matthew 25). On the last day, the righteous
judge will separate humanity, sheep to the right, goats to the
left. The basis? The ones on His right—the saved ones—were
selected because they fed the hungry, gave drink to the thirsty,
cared for the stranger, clothed the naked, and visited the
imprisoned. Those who didn't, the goats, were cursed and sent
"into the eternal fire prepared for the devil and his angels." No
excuses accepted.

To help Moses grasp that no explanation would excuse him,
the Lord gave him Aaron as his mouthpiece, promised to provide the words himself, and urged him to pick up his miracle-
making staff and get on with it. "You may not feel like doing it,
Moses, but I have called you. I have heard your excuses. They
don't wash. Now—up and at it."

Alexander Whyte, the canny Scottish parson whose wisdom
still inspires preachers today, once prayed for a student lying ill
and weak in a back room in Edinburgh. "O Lord," he said,
"Thou givest the victory unto the weak! We give it to the strong

and to the talented, but Thou givest it unto the weak. Amen." Since God gives the victory to the weak, then only the weak need apply.

In his own eyes, Moses was weak. He was convinced he was not up to the assignment. He knew all too well the plight of his people in Egypt. His ears were not deaf to their cries. He just didn't want the responsibility.

Fortunately for Israel's sake—and our own—we have not yet come to the end of the story.

8

Bugs, Boils, and Blackness

Exodus 5:1–10:29

"Why should I believe in your God? What evidence can you produce that will convince me your god is GOD? So you can do a few miracles. So what? In my court, I have at my disposal wise men, magicians, astrologers. I give the order and they produce the miracle. That's what the unwashed masses think they are, anyway. I understand that these men are really manipulators of appearances. They can conjure up a new reality to impress and control. I use them when it's convenient for me. No, don't think you can force me to give in to your demands with your pathetic kind of hocus-pocus. Do you understand? I don't believe in your god."

Pharaoh Challenges Moses

This was Pharaoh's response to Moses, which became Moses and Aaron's challenge. It was a double dare, really. They had to convince Pharaoh to believe in them. To believe they were telling the truth, that they were who they said they were and could do what they said they could. That was the first challenge. The second was even greater: to get him to believe in their God.

It would take some doing. Pharaoh was well acquainted with these Hebrew people. There was nothing about them for him to admire. They were a herd of slaves, the dregs of Egyptian society. Free labor. Expendable energy. He had nothing to fear from them. Nor from their God. If He were so powerful, why were they so pitifully weak? In this contest of wills, the odds were all on Pharaoh's side.

So from his point of view, there was nothing to be gained by believing Moses and Aaron and everything to lose if the Hebrews should slip out of his grasp. (This is not a bad lesson for us to remember, is it, we who would like to convert our friends and neighbors to Christ? Why should they change? Why should they believe? What's in it for *them*? These are their questions, and they are legitimate ones.)

Malcolm Muggeridge, the famous British television commentator, believed in God many years before he gave in and became a Christian. He admitted, as a matter of fact, that he would have preferred that God didn't exist. His temperament was much better suited to what this world offers, he thought. He wished he could have dismissed the existence and purpose of God as only somebody's wishful thinking, or maybe a man-made symbol of self-importance. He wrote in *Jesus Rediscovered* that while he never wanted or feared or felt under any necessity for God, he was unfortunately driven to the conclusion that God wanted him. So after years of procrastination, he finally capitulated. God got him.

In some ways, Muggeridge was a latter-day pharaoh but without a kingdom. The Egyptian king also never wanted or feared or felt the necessity to invent any other god. Since he considered himself to be the son of the sun god, this God the Hebrews chattered about had to be an imposter.

Moses Answers the Challenge

So Moses began slowly, methodically laying down the case for God. He offered proof. He showed Pharaoh a staff that metamorphosed into a snake, and then turned the snake loose to swallow up the court magicians' staffs. It was a good show, but it didn't do the trick. It wasn't special. Pharaoh's magicians could, in fact, perform such magic. The leprous hand trick didn't impress him much, either. As for turning the Nile River into blood? Pretty impressive performance, but once more to no effect. "The Egyptian magicians did the same thing by their secret arts, and Pharaoh's heart became hard" (Exodus 7:22).

So Moses and Aaron summoned the frogs, and soon they overran the place. Disgusting, maybe, but not convincing, because "the magicians did the same things by their secret arts; they also made frogs come up on the land of Egypt" (8:7).

But when Moses summoned the gnats that darkened the sky with their soaring, the magicians were stumped. They understood the black arts, but this was more than anything they had ever seen. "The magicians said to Pharaoh, 'This is the finger of God'" (8:19). They were impressed, ready to concede the contest, but Pharaoh wasn't. His heart became like stone. He would not listen, "just as the LORD had said." The contest narrowed now. The magicians faded. They knew when they'd been bested, but Pharaoh didn't.

Convincing Skeptics

The story we are studying is old, but the problem is modern. How do you convince a skeptic? Many modern intellectuals are descendants of Karl Marx, whose materialistic determinism (as embodied in various forms of communism) captured the mind of so much of the twentieth-century world. And of Sigmund Freud, who taught that God is merely a human projection, a

phantasm constructed of our deepest fears and yearnings. And
of Friedrich Nietzsche, who presumed to announce the death
of God. And of Charles Darwin, whose evolutionary explanation of human origins left no room for God. And of A.J. Ayer,
who declared "all utterances about the nature of God are non-
sensical." And of Bertrand Russell, who insisted that "what science cannot tell us, mankind cannot know." It wasn't all that
long ago that the Death of God theologians were presiding
over God's funeral, their eulogies including the words of
Algernon Swinburne, who wrote in the nineteenth century:

> Thou art smitten, thou God,
> thou art smitten;
> thy death is upon thee, O Lord.
> And the love-song of earth as thou diest
> resounds through the wind of her wings—
> Glory to Man in the highest! For Man is the master of
>   things.

How would you speak to us descendants of these thinkers,
Moses? What arguments would you muster to persuade us to
believe in your God instead of in their pronouncements? What
miracles would you perform to convince us to believe? With
such a host of thinkers arrayed against you, why should we
take your claims seriously, Moses?

The truth, of course, is that millions of people do take
Moses' God very seriously, or want to. Their hearts are not
completely encrusted. But they won't be persuaded, any more
than Pharaoh was, by gimmicks or sleight of hand. They won't
be moved by snakes swallowing other snakes, or river water
turning to blood, or by summoned plagues of frogs or gnats.
Not magic, but something else, something far less flashy, is
what people seek. It hasn't escaped their notice that in the
twenty-first century, in spite of the thunderings of this host of
God-dismissing intellectuals, God still hasn't died. There are
too many other voices testifying to His existence. The very

sciences that once seemed poised to overthrow God now present arguments that force us to rethink God's existence. People have come to realize that there is probably more evidence for the existence of God than for the subatomic particles on which contemporary physics rests. We believe these particles exist, though we've never seen them, because we see their effects. We believe in God on the same basis.

Convincing Others: A Personal Testimony

When I first began preaching in the late 1950s, I had to face what Moses faced but on a much smaller scale. My adversary was not a great king, but the people in my section of Portland, Oregon, whom I hoped to persuade to follow Jesus. Would they believe me? Why should they believe me? How could I convince them? And what kind of programs should the new church I was establishing offer? Would people be attracted by our Christian education program? By pastoral counseling? By the busing programs that were so popular then? By eloquence in the pulpit? If I could get them to listen, what should I tell them?

I felt so inexperienced, so inadequate, so unconvincing. The little church met in a tiny building that offered nothing of beauty to behold. Why should anyone come to hear a greenhorn preacher in a plain little building with almost no programs to offer?

Yet from that humble start grew a strong, vibrant congregation. People did come and they did listen. They came to hear and stayed because they believed. Somehow I was able to persuade them to trust in God.

My arguments weren't really from theology. The church's attractiveness wasn't in its music, or recreation or entertainment; it certainly wasn't in its preaching. In fact, my insecurities in those days were heightened by something I read in the *Interpreter's Bible*, a respected commentary set of the day. "The athletic minister who plays good baseball with his boys and bears with all the old golfing reprobates of his town in the links has a more responsive audience when he speaks out on religion or righteousness than has the old mufflered bookworm who shuffles over the parish in galoshes." That hit me because I didn't play baseball and still don't golf and was, even in those early days, a young mufflered bookworm shuffling over my parish in galoshes. ("Dad, you really were a nerd, weren't you?" my kids later asked. I was.)

No, what happened in that little church is what we're going to see eventually happening in Moses' confrontation with Pharaoh. Over time, the case for God was built. People learned more and more about Him as they studied the Bible, and they liked what they learned. They saw that the power wasn't in their untried preacher but in the Word he was doing his best to explain. They began to experience something of God's love and power in their own lives; they fell into the embrace of His grace and the love of the congregation.

Powerful Convictions

Two convictions emerge from our reading of this passage, two convictions that also emerged in my Moses-like experience in that little church so long ago.

There Is Power in Servitude

The first is that there is power in servitude. The real struggle for Pharaoh wasn't a theological one. It was all about money. "It's the economy, stupid," Bill Clinton chanted in his 1992 presidential bid. Egypt's economy would be powerfully impacted if the Hebrew labor force escaped. Pharaoh wasn't just being asked to let them go worship God; he was being asked to take a serious hit in his income. They were the servants; the economy rested on their backs. Jesus was right in the Beatitudes: "Blessed are the meek, for they will inherit the earth." They are already the force that runs it. Kings and emperors rise and fall, but the meek till the soil and build the buildings and oil the economy. There is power in servitude.

There Is Weakness in Power

This is the second conviction: The might of the powerful is less than it seems. As we shall see, all the king's horses and all the king's men couldn't keep Pharaoh's kingdom from tumbling once God had spoken. The plagues were too much, even for the king. He should have learned the always-relevant advice that Paul passes on in Galatians 6:7: "Do not be deceived: God cannot be mocked. A man reaps what he sows."

A couple of decades ago, I was teaching a course on the New Testament church at Haus Edelweiss, a Christian teaching mission at Heilegenkreuz, just outside of Vienna, Austria. In those days, the Iron Curtain was firmly in place. My students came from Poland, Yugoslavia, and Hungary. Their bravery in coming and their thirst to know God's Word were inspiring. In the midst of the course, my admiration for my students soared. Being citizens of communist nations, they had risked much to study the Bible. They were living reminders of what a subversive power God's Word is. For two thousand years, Christians have met in graveyards and cathedrals, in hovels and mansions, in free democracies and totalitarian tyrannies, to hear the Word of the Lord. No government has been able to stamp out these meetings once and for all. The church has outlasted the mighty Roman Empire and all other empires, monarchies, fiefdoms, duchies, and other regimes that have opposed it. The mighty have been brought low and the humble exalted, and as Paul counseled, they reaped what they sowed. As for Pharaoh, he was clearly on the wrong side of this contest.

Lessons Learned From Pharaoh's Palace

A Lesson in Government

When historian Barbara Tuchman published *The March of Folly*, I knew I had to read the book. The title itself is a grabber. I suspected it would be an historical overview of stupid mistakes that governments make. I was right. It was an intriguing read. Tuchman is pretty hard on what she calls rulers' "woodenheadedness." She details the amazing aptitude for self-deception that drives monarchs and presidents to move immovable objects and resist irresistible forces. Instead of striving to see their situations clearly, woodenheaded sovereigns close their eyes to warning signals and their ears to cautionary counsel. What they want it to be, will be. Regardless. So Pharaoh could comfort himself that he was in—well, we can't really call it "good" company, can we? At least he wasn't the only king who ever paid dearly for his hardness of heart. Still, for all his stubborn willfulness, the contest didn't go his way.

- After the first plague of blood, Pharaoh promised nothing. His magicians would do as well.
- After the frogs, Pharaoh promised, then reneged.
- After the flies, he promised to let the people go sacrifice in the desert, a three-day journey. Again, he reneged.
- After the others, he negotiated.
- After the locusts, he promised that the Israelite men could go, but no one else.
- After the darkness, the men, women, and children could go, but no flocks or herds.

And the refrain kept repeating itself, the words weaving themselves through the narrative: *hardened heart*. Tuchman would call it "woodenheadedness."

Call it what you will, the result is loss.

We are still assessing the cost of America's failure to face reality in Vietnam. The most widely quoted remark of that war tells it all: "It becomes necessary to destroy the town in order to save it." This was an American officer's explanation for wiping out a village of innocent women and children. Perhaps you can make some sense of the sentence. I can't. It's one more exhibit, it seems to me, along with so many other so-called justifications from ravaged battlefields all over the world, that woodenheadedness is in the saddle and rides mankind.

Even Pharaoh's officials could see what he would not see. After the plague of hail, they begged him, "How long will this man be a snare to us? Let the people go, so that they may worship the LORD their God. Do you not yet realize that Egypt is ruined?" (Exodus 10:7). Their wisdom prevailed, for the moment, but then Pharaoh had a better idea. Leave the women and children. Just the men could go, he said, still trying to manipulate the negotiations in his favor. He would not see that he was up against a power far greater than his own.

A more contemporary lesson can be drawn from the current plight of Russia. Throughout most of the twentieth century, Russian rulers starting with Lenin and Stalin and continuing through Khrushchev and Brezhnev boasted of their country's superior power. Communism would bury capitalism, the East would soon rule over the West, and the Kremlin would lead the world. Today, the Soviet Union is shattered, the Russian economy is in ruins, and its old enemy the United States is unchallenged as the single world power (although its other primary competitor, China, is on the ascendancy). In the once-proud Soviet Union, woodenheadedness has unfortunately conquered again.

Of course, we are reading Hebrew history long after the fact. From the king's point of view, we have it all wrong. He was Pharaoh, after all, a god in his own right. And he had everything: armies, treasure-filled cities, rich and fertile fields. And this Moses? He had nothing. He was nobody. He was the leader of a people of nobodies. Slaves.

But those slaves had God. Having nothing but God, they had everything. Pharaoh just couldn't—because he wouldn't—see it.

A Lesson in Negotiating With God

This is the point that Pharaoh missed. He thought he was negotiating with Moses, when in fact he was dealing with God.

After each concession, he thought the negotiations were over. He gave a little, modified his position somewhat, and undoubtedly congratulated himself on his subtlety. But it wasn't over. He could have used Churchill's insight. When General Eisenhower led the Allies in their successful invasion of Algeria and Morocco, the British people cheered. The prime minister cautioned them to hold off their celebration. It wasn't over. "This is not the end, it is not even the beginning of the end. But it is, perhaps, the end of the beginning." He knew what additional sacrifices lay ahead if the evils of Nazism and Fascism were to be laid to rest. The Allies had already declared that this war had to be fought to the enemy's unconditional surrender. You don't compromise with evil.

Moses was in no mood for compromise, either. He was speaking on behalf of God, and God would not be satisfied with less than Pharaoh's complete capitulation. But the king went on complimenting himself on his negotiation skills, fudging just a little here, giving in a little there, still confident he had the upper hand. He was not yet ready to do the one thing Moses required: "Let my people go."

It's the one thing a despot can't do.

Here's another famous example. In April 1492, the powerful Lorenzo the Magnificent, who had held all of Florence in his sway, was dying. In his final days, he turned to God. He summoned Savonarola to his palatial villa near Florence. The prior of the Dominican monastery was the one churchman Lorenzo had never been able to bribe or scare. Not surprisingly, then, Savonarola was the one Lorenzo called for his last rites.

Savonarola hurried to Lorenzo's side. He told him he would grant Lorenzo his blessing on three conditions. First, he must exercise his faith in Jesus Christ as sole ground for his forgiveness. Lorenzo agreed.

Second, he must restore all the estates he had dishonestly wrested from the citizens of Florence. Again, Lorenzo agreed.

Third, he must restore to the people of the city the freedom they enjoyed before Lorenzo's family (the despotic Medicis) grabbed all power. At this, he hesitated, turned to face the wall, and died. The one thing he could not give up, even on his deathbed, was his power over the people.

I can't read Lorenzo's story without remembering King Herod (whom some scholars believe was already mortally ill) tightening his chokehold on Judea and ordering the slaughter of the innocents to destroy any potential successor to his throne. We wouldn't even know about Herod, however, if it hadn't been for the baby whose birth so frightened him. How do you account for the kind of woodenheadedness that could delude a dying Lorenzo or Herod into believing he could hang on to power, anyway?

What advice could we give Pharaoh? Just exactly what is the best method for negotiating with God? What do we say to the man who believed he was protecting Egypt's economy, his own honor, and, today's politicians would say, national security?

Our best advice would have to be this: As a rule, it is best not to negotiate with God. (I know, I know—Pharaoh could always bring up the example of Abraham's argument on behalf of Sodom and Gomorrah, or Moses' pleading for God to spare Israel, but basing your case on the exception is not the most prudent of strategies.) Our counsel would be . . . well, that's the third lesson.

A Lesson in Repentance

What God is after is Pharaoh's genuine, full-hearted cooperation. That means a change of mind. A genuine change of mind, resulting in different behavior. It's called repentance, and among the powerful it is very rare. You would think that when a king's strategy fails him, he would adopt a new plan. As Tuchman explains it, however, the more common response is not a new plan but renewed "woodenheadedness."

As Pharaoh's resistance deepened, we are struck by these strange words: "The LORD hardened Pharaoh's heart" (Exodus 9:12). The Lord's role didn't appear in the instances of the blood, frogs, gnats, flies, livestock (the first five plagues), or hail. But when we read of the boils, locusts, and darkness, we also read that Pharaoh's heart was hardened—by the Lord.

Earlier in the contest, when he pleaded with Moses to get rid of the frogs, Pharaoh almost sounded like a believer. "Pray to the LORD to take the frogs away from me and my people, and I will let your people go to offer sacrifices to the LORD" (Exodus 8:8).

After the frogs died, though, Pharaoh "hardened his heart and would not listen to Moses and Aaron" (8:15). So the Lord sent the gnats, but without results. Then the flies. This time Pharaoh conceded: "Go, sacrifice to your God here in the land" (8:25). Conceded they could worship, but not that they could leave Egypt. But when the flies were gone, once again Pharaoh hardened his heart ("woodened-up" his head!) and reneged on his promise. This led to the livestock plague, "yet his heart was unyielding and he would not let the people go" (9:7). On to the boils. This time the language changes. Now it was the Lord who hardened Pharaoh's heart.

It appears at first as if Pharaoh was beginning to catch on. After the hail, he cried out, "This time I have sinned. The LORD is in the right, and I and my people are in the wrong" (9:27). He promised to let them go.

Until the hail stopped.

Now God stepped in. "I have hardened his heart and the hearts of his officials so that I may perform these miraculous signs of mine among them" (10:1). It was too late for Pharaoh now. He had ceded control to the evil in his heart.

Most of us take comfort in the promise of Psalm 37:4— "Delight yourself in the Lord and he will give you the desires of your heart."

There is a dark side to this verse, however, one that is equally true: "Delight yourself in almost anything, and you will receive the desires of your heart."

It is the lesson taught in Alcoholics Anonymous. If alcohol is your god, alcohol will give you what you think you want. If drugs have become your god, then drugs will give you the desires of your heart. If power, you will delight in the exercise of it. The goal of AA is to help alcoholics learn a new delight.

They call it serving a higher power. But you will not serve the higher power until you repent of serving the former one.

The only hope for Pharaoh and his people was a change of heart. Repentance.

I mentioned Russian rulers earlier. One of them wrote his memoirs. In *Khrushchev Remembers,* Stalin's hardness of heart is illustrated. After a World War II engagement that cost Russia thousands of soldiers, Stalin called Khrushchev back from the front. He dreaded going, because he was afraid he'd have to take the blame personally for the disaster. Stalin had overruled his attempts to call off the offensive, but that didn't matter. "For Stalin to have agreed that we had been right when we halted the operation would have meant admitting his own mistake. And that sort of nobility was not for him. He would stop at nothing to avoid taking the responsibility for something that had gone wrong."[34]

"Do you not yet realize that Egypt is ruined?" Pharaoh's advisors cried. But there would be no yielding. Pharaoh could not be wrong. He was not responsible. He would not repent.

How unusual it is for a politician or government leader, even in our free country, to admit, "I was wrong. It was my fault. I am sorry." Or a corporate executive. Or, for that matter, anybody else.

Somebody pointed out to me that John the Baptist didn't entice people to his riverside church service by intoning, "Smile! God loves you." No, his message was, "Repent, for the kingdom of heaven is near" (Matthew 3:2). It's time for a reality check. No more woodenheadedness. No more proud hardness of heart.

Jesus picked up where John left off. His message was not, "I'm OK, you're OK." Instead, He repeated John's very words.

Peter, on the Day of Pentecost, didn't throw open the doors of the church by preaching, "Something good is going to happen to you today." To the contrary, he urged people to save themselves from a corrupt generation. He pressed them to repent.

You can't escape the impression when you read the Scriptures that repentance is nonnegotiable. The good news, though, is that it's possible. You don't have to be ruled by your own stubbornness. I heard of a wonderful sermon title: "U-Turns Permitted."

That's the message here. U-turns are permitted. Don't waste your time and effort trying to defend your past. You don't have to live in it either. Unlike Pharaoh, you don't have to keep on repeating your mistakes, digging yourself deeper and deeper into trouble. U-turns *are* permitted.

Governments make such mistakes. They feel they can't turn back, can't admit some policy errors, can't repent. National honor is at stake. We can't let God's people go!

Persons make the same mistake. "I can't change. I can't admit I have been wrong. I don't want anybody to think that I was weak or misled or sinful."

The best advice? It's Peter's, in Acts 3:19, "Repent, then, and turn to God, so that your sins may be wiped out, that times of refreshing may come from the Lord." We can't rewrite history. It is meaningless to speculate about what might have happened if Pharaoh had repented, although we can't help thinking what "times of refreshing" would have come to the Egyptian homes that did not lose their children and the soldiers of Pharaoh who would not have drowned in the sea.

As I said, speculating on the "what ifs" of history isn't very productive. But considering what happens to people who repent is. What if your sins were blotted out? What if you had nothing to fear? What if your shame, your sense of guilt, your embarrassment, your fears were replaced by "times of refreshing [that] come from the Lord"?

It doesn't pay to negotiate with God, that we have seen.

But to trust and obey? There really is no other way, is there?

9

Something to Remember You By

Exodus 11:1–12:42

Memories Define Us

As a Christian whose worship is centered on another Feast of Remembrance—variously called the Lord's table, Holy Communion, or the Eucharist—reading Exodus 11 and 12 so many centuries after the Passover is a reminder of how much memory defines us. Without memory, I am nobody. My sense of identity is an amalgamation of memories, sifted and sorted by my values and perceptions. Ask me who I am and I'll tell you what I remember.

What is true of individuals is true of nations as well, although nations sometimes have difficulty remembering who they are. Our national holidays, for example, were established with an outburst of enthusiasm and a rash of good intentions; in time, they disintegrate into little more than days off work that we devote to playing, sleeping, overeating, and drinking. Think of Memorial Day (do you remember what it memorializes?), Labor Day (what's it about?), and even Thanksgiving.

And what patriotism is left for Independence Day? Or Veterans Day (which veterans, of what war)? The national memory is short, shortest of all when the times are good and the living is easy.

In fact, the only national holidays Americans as a rule celebrate with faithfulness to their original meanings are Christmas and Easter. Of course, in our pluralistic society, these special days are more secular than holy. Yet American Christians by and large are determined to teach the "reasons for the seasons" to the next generation. We want our children to remember.

Memory also defines Jews. Harry Golden, a twentieth-century writer, offers this insight: "Historically anyone born to a Jewish mother is a Jew whether the father is Jewish or not. The mother is a Jew because it is she who maintains the Sabbath so the men can worship. God told Moses, 'There is a magnificent gift in my treasure chamber and its name is Sabbath and I shall give it to Israel.' The Sabbath is a time of joy, the streets and the workshops still, the home filled with celebration and reverence. The Sabbath is probably the secret of the Jew's survival."[35] Add his comments to those of James A. Pike, who concluded that "a Jew is one who remembers, who remembers two things: the bondage in Egypt and the exodus through the Red Sea waters."[36] Pike says Jews are what they remember; Golden says they are held together by their days of remembering.

Like Christians, they remember on a special day each week in addition to the dedicated holidays (holy days) throughout the year. Whether at their principal feasts such as Passover and Unleavened Bread or in their weekly observance of the Sabbath, Jews get together to celebrate what they remember and in so doing, are reminded of who they are. In this respect, Christians are certainly their close relatives for when we gather, whether at Easter or Christmas or at the Lord's table on Sunday, our purpose is also to remember who we are and how we got this way. This is the essence of community.

Community. That's the word Rabbi Harold Kushner employs to define who Jews are. He says that in this respect,

Jews are unlike Christians, who always start with what we believe. Jews can't agree on dogma, he writes, "because Jewish identity is not centered in belief. It is centered in community and history." What binds Jews together, he insists, "is that we were a people before we had a religion. Christianity begins with an idea—the incarnation of God in Jesus, the crucifixion and resurrection of Jesus as a way of redeeming man from sin. If a person believes that idea, he is a Christian." First they believe; then the believers form communities of belief. Jews, on the other hand, were a community first, beginning with the families of Abraham, Isaac, and Jacob. Then they were formed finally and indivisibly by their exodus experience into a nation with an unforgettable past.[37]

These insights help us grasp the importance of the events we have been studying: bondage in Egypt, liberation through the Passover, the forming of a new nation. Without these experiences, and the memory of these experiences, who would the Jews be?

A birth in Bethlehem, a crucifixion in Jerusalem, a resurrection from the tomb, an ascension into Heaven—without these events, and the memory of these events, who would Christians be?

The Passover—Something Jews Never Forget

The Story Behind the Passover

Moses' prolonged negotiations with the Egyptian king graphically illustrate what a difference perspective makes. We turn to the Scriptures to learn more about the people of God; the descendants of Abraham, Isaac, and Jacob; the kinfolk of the noble Joseph himself. We're on their side in this study because the biblical account focuses our attention on them. They, not Pharaoh and his court, are our ancestors. To probe their experience is to learn more about ourselves.

That's *our* perspective, but it wasn't Pharaoh's. To him, these forebears of ours were, as we have repeatedly noted, just a herd of slaves, dirty and dull. They were, to be certain, valuable property, the backbone of his economy, but of no individual worth. Collectively, they constituted a great economic asset. But God's people? No way.

Israel's God did not share Pharaoh's viewpoint, of course. Never were Moses' people out of His line of vision; His eye watched over them and His heart cared for them. Remember Exodus 2:23-25?

> During that long period, the king of Egypt died. The Israelites groaned in their slavery and cried out, and their cry for help because of their slavery went up to God. God heard their groaning and he remembered his covenant with Abraham, with Isaac and with Jacob. So God looked on the Israelites and was concerned about them.

That's when He presented himself in the burning bush to Moses and dispatched Moses to the king with His imperative, "Let my people go."

Pharaoh wouldn't let them go, so, as we have seen, God released a string of plagues to persuade Pharaoh, but the ruler's heart just became progressively harder. Then came the final blow—the plague of the firstborn. The king's stubbornness cost his people dearly as death struck the Egyptian firstborns from the greatest household to the humblest.

The Israelites who obeyed God were spared.

Obedience. Scripturally speaking, salvation and obedience are inseparable. Look closely at how particular the Lord's instructions were. He intended to be obeyed. The time for action was in the month of Abib (that is, late March or early April). But not just anytime in Abib: They were to begin preparations on the tenth day of the month of Abib. On that day, they were to carry out the following instructions (Exodus 12:3-11):

1. The head of each household was to select a year-old male lamb or kid.

2. He was to slay the sacrificial animal at twilight on the fourteenth day and apply the blood to the doorframe of his house.
3. Each family was to eat the roasted lamb or kid along with bitter herbs and unleavened bread.
4. The meat was not only to be roasted, but also roasted whole with head and legs intact and its washed entrails inside. Nothing was to be eaten raw or after being boiled in water.
5. There could be no leftovers. Whatever was uneaten was to be burnt.
6. They were to eat the meal as if in haste: robes tucked into belts, sandals on feet, and staffs in hand.

So much for the Passover event itself. The passage moves on to instructions for the annual Feast of Unleavened Bread—from the event to the future remembering of the event. Here the same attention was given to particulars: eat unleavened bread for seven days, remember Israel's hasty departure from Egypt, and be pure and uncorrupt (as unleavened bread is "uncorrupted" by yeast that works its way throughout the dough). God's instructions left little room for today's popular "whatever" attitude.

The Meaning of Passover Today

Thus it was in the beginning. Today, thousands of years later, when Jewish children ask, "What does this ceremony mean to you?" their elders answer, "It is the Passover sacrifice to the Lord, who passed over the houses of the Israelites in Egypt and spared our homes when He struck down the Egyptians." It is their way of saying, "We observe this feast 'lest we forget.'"

When I was the pastor of Central Christian Church in Mesa, we invited a leader of Jews for Jesus to be with us for the Agape Feast we held each Thursday evening before Easter. Our members filled our fellowship hall for the celebration and listened carefully as our guest took us through each stage of the

Passover meal, recalling for us those events so long ago when the Lord delivered the Israelites from Egypt and directed Moses as he led them to freedom. We ate roasted lamb with bitter herbs and unleavened bread, we prayed, we remembered.

That we asked a Jewish Christian to lead us through this celebration offended the local rabbi. He was angry when he telephoned me. He felt we had desecrated the Seder meal. We should not have had a Christian, even if he did claim to be a Jew, taking us through this sacred Jewish feast. "But," I tried to explain, "it is *our* feast too. Our Christian roots go back like yours to ancient Egypt, and beyond Egypt to Abraham, and beyond Abraham to Adam. It is as imperative that we remember our roots as it is that you remember yours. As a matter of fact, we find our relationship with one another in this common history." I didn't pacify him, and I was sorry. We Christians must not forget either.

Ours is a memory of God in action. In Egypt, He acted to save an enslaved people. In the New Testament, the emphasis becomes more personal, as 2 Peter 3:9 makes clear: "He [the Lord] is patient with you, not wanting anyone to perish, but everyone [each individual person] to come to repentance." His goal in Egypt was to save the nation of Israel. He did save all who obeyed. His goal today is to save everyone, and He does save those who repent. Throughout this study, we have been impressed with God's proactivity. He moves and shakes and saves. He does not suffer suffering gladly! We dare not forget.

Communion—Something Christians Never Forget

Most Christians can recall their first Communion. Many of us will gladly recount special Communion services when we felt more keenly than usual the presence of the Lord and the oneness of the body of Christ. None of us would fail to be touched by the Chang family's unusual celebration in 1981, because the family's sense of joy is at the heart of our celebrations as well.

Paul Chang gathered up his wife and two children from their home in Southeast Asia to meet his family in China. When they had assembled, there were twenty-one of them in all, among them some Paul had never met before. It was an especially emotional reunion for Grandma Chang, who was eighty-three and had suffered grievously since her pastor husband had been imprisoned and brutalized. He died in prison of malnutrition. She survived his death, but life was very hard.

But now Mrs. Chang had her family together and great was her rejoicing. On their final day together, they observed a family Communion service. The Communionware was the lid from a tin box of cookies; an inexpensive handkerchief covered it. Broken cookies represented Christ's body, sugar cane juice His blood.

Grandma Chang wept and prayed, "O Lord, it has been so long. For more than twenty years I haven't been able to take Communion. We've not been able to remember Your broken body and the blood as You commanded. Oh, thank You that You allowed me to live to see this day. At last we've been able to come to Your table again."[38]

My family could identify with the Changs. We certainly have not suffered as they have, nor have we had long periods of enforced separation. Because we are now scattered, though, with our children and grandchildren in several states, when we get together we observe certain rituals—lest we forget. We devote the close of almost every evening of our annual all-family vacation to storytelling. Certain events must be recounted: when David drowned Jeff's jeep in Cultus Lake; when Brian jumped on his friend Joel's bed to wake him up—only to discover that it wasn't Joel sleeping there, but his grandmother; when I walked through the closed patio door at Kim and Bob's house, with disastrous results; when Candy had to be carried out of the cave on a stretcher after she and Julie thought they'd hide and scare the rest of us as we inched our way along in the darkness; when the newly married Joy burned the chicken in the pressure cooker and raised such a stink in the church building we were living in that the leaders decided we should have a parsonage. And on and on. New stories get added, of course, but we always rehearse the old ones. We don't want to forget them. They define us.

And then there is Christmas Eve. For years now, we have all been together for Christmas. We go to church as a large family and take over one of the candlelit Communion tables. We hold hands, pray together, and partake of the bread and the cup. Cherished, cherished ritual. Lest we forget.

Why is Communion so vital a part of Christian worship? Perhaps the best answer is in an old hymn, "Lead Me to Calvary":

> King of my life I crown Thee now—
> Thine shall the glory be;
> Lest I forget thy thorn-crowned brow,
> Lead me to Calvary.
>
> Lest I forget Gethsemane,
> Lest I forget Thine agony,
> Lest I forget Thy love for me,
> Lead me to Calvary.

In Communion, a Christian remembers Christ's suffering in Gethsemane, His agony on the cross, God's incalculable love for unworthy human beings like us. Earlier I asked, "Who is a Jew?" Now it's time to ask, "What is a Christian?" Like the Jews who are defined by their memory of the Passover and Exodus, we are defined by our memory of—and commitment never to forget—Calvary, the death and resurrection of Christ. Every Lord's Day, and on the special holy days Good Friday and Easter, we remember. And we remember the same God the Jews remember, believing that He who delivered the people of God from bondage in Egypt later delivered "whosoever will" from bondage in sin.

The Passover lamb was slain to save the firstborn Israelites. Jesus, the Lamb of God, was slain to save not just the Israelites, but all persons who call on Him.

More Than "Just Symbols"

I hope I'm communicating that the exodus and the cross of Christ have long been symbols of God's saving grace. I need to make certain, though, that you don't think I'm saying of either one that it's "just a symbol." Perhaps this warning isn't needed any longer in these post-September 11th days. The collapse of the World Trade Center and the attack on the Pentagon have entered America's consciousness as terrible symbols of terrorism. Nobody refers to them as "just symbols." And the picture of President Bush standing at Ground Zero holding high the American flag is permanently etched on our brains as the symbol of American resilience and determination. For us, his action, permanently captured on film, will never be "just a symbol."

Symbols are not mere signs pointing to something else; rather, they contain or evoke something of the power of the thing they symbolize. I mentioned the flag. People have died for that flag. The flag has rallied others to sacrificial service for their fellow citizens. Consider the firefighters and police in New York in the weeks and months following the terrorist attack or the armed servicemen and women serving under that flag on foreign battlefields. That's why we are so deeply offended if we see someone stepping on or otherwise desecrating a flag. Following September 11th, the star-spangled banners were flying on the lawns and from houses and office buildings all over America, even waving on cars and trucks driving by. Little children drew and colored paper flags to give to their neighbors. Symbolic, but not "just symbols."

Think of the awards presented at athletic contests, or of grown men crying as they receive the World Series trophy. These are symbols, these wreaths and ribbons and cups—but never "just symbols."

In the tumultuous 1960s, rebellious young people burned their draft cards. Were they just setting a match to cardboard? Not to the veterans of America's wars.

I could keep going, couldn't I? What does it symbolize when you turn someone's picture to the wall? When you drive out to the cemetery to visit the gravesite of a loved one? When you hand back an engagement ring?

A person's name, of course, is a symbol. Mention a familiar name and the very speaking of it conjures up the image of the person, our feelings about him or her, memories of shared experiences, either positive or negative. I could write your name here. On one level, it is just some inked dots stamped on white paper. But if you read your name here, that's not what it would signify to you. Or to me, if we were acquainted. No, your name would not be "just a symbol."

Symbols of God's Power

Pharaoh caught on that for the Israelites, the permission they were seeking to worship in their own way was about something more than worship. Up until then, when Pharaoh had given his permission for the Hebrews to leave—only to immediately rescind or place unacceptable restrictions on his permission—he had said, "Go, worship the LORD your God" (10:8, 24) or "Go, sacrifice to your God" (8:25). But this time, it was, "Up! Leave my people!" (12:31). He had finally caught on. He was in a contest he couldn't win. There would be no more deception, no more manipulation, no more power struggle. At least, that was his intent at the moment. "Go, you win! This isn't really just about worship, is it? It's about who you are. It's your declaration of independence. It's about a God who is greater than me." That's why he added this surprise: "Bless me."

> During the night Pharaoh summoned Moses and Aaron and said, "Up! Leave my people, you and the Israelites! Go, worship the LORD as you have requested. Take your flocks and herds, as you have said, and go. And also bless me" (Exodus 12:31, 32).

Pharaoh, the supreme ruler of the Egyptian world, entreated Moses for a blessing. Yet it was not really Moses' blessing he wanted. Throughout this contest, Moses had made it very clear that he was only God's spokesman. He had no power in himself. Pharaoh knew that. There was more to this capitulation than meets the eye. As we have pointed out before, Pharaoh was no ordinary king. In Egypt's theology, he was the son of god. This was not some government official asking a holy man for a blessing; this was a god asking Moses' God to look favorably on him. It was the head of the world's greatest nation admitting his defeat, seeking the favor of his conqueror. His people and herds were dying. He couldn't restore them. Please Moses, bless me.

He did change his mind, as you know. But this was a moment to be remembered. He was not dealing with a mere shepherd. His antagonist was not some agent or representation ("just a symbol") of a higher power. God himself had been acting through the "symbols" of Moses' power. These plagues were not Moses' doing. Pharaoh had been dealing with God himself.

Celebrating Communion—A Foretaste of Heaven

Let me jump from the Israelite experience to the Christian meaning of Communion again. Christians in the early centuries of the faith insisted on two things. They wanted to be able to celebrate Communion together, and they wanted *not* to be forced to worship the emperor. They were pretty easy to get along with otherwise, but on these two matters they would not budge. They wouldn't even perform the compromise the emperor offered—that of casting a perfunctory pinch of incense in the imperial temple. Why not? the baffled emperor wondered. They would not because of what that seemingly harmless act symbolized. For them, it was comparable to our saluting the American flag. It was a form of pledging allegiance, and Christians could not pledge allegiance to more than one God. It was not "just a symbol."

Many, in fact, died because of their refusal to conform to the emperor's wishes. They died because they understood how symbols work. By casting incense in the imperial temple, they were acknowledging the emperor as Lord and God. Christians believed only Christ could legitimately wear those titles. So they took their symbolic stand: They would not toss a pinch of incense into the fire.

They were equally stubborn about their positive symbolic statement. Rome's rulers had difficulty understanding why Christians would rather die than give up weekly Communion, also. These fervent disciples gathered each week to affirm the lordship of Jesus, to remember His sacrifice on the cross for them, and to give thanks for their salvation. It was a simple ceremony, this partaking of just a little wine, just a little bread. But it was never "just a symbol." Then, when their Communion time was over, they took the leftover bread and wine to the sick and shut-in members of their congregation, so they, too, could have fellowship with the Lord and with other Christians. Their participation symbolized the wholeness of the body of Christ. No one was left out. Communion symbolized community in Christ.

Two millennia after those earliest Christians braved the wrath of an emperor to observe Communion, this simple service remains the church's central ceremony of remembrance. Bill Hook, a member of our congregation in Mesa, thanks God for an especially memorable Communion experience in his family. One Sunday in his home church, Bill's father, who was not scheduled to give the Communion meditation that day, substituted for an absent fellow elder. Mr. Hook spoke briefly about how we must always be ready since we don't know when our Lord may call us home. He said what a glorious day it will be when we see God in His throne room. When he finished speaking, he returned to his seat, took Communion himself, and died. He was gone within a minute or two. You can't convince his family that this last Communion with his church family was "just a symbol." God was in that moment. He was giving them a foretaste on earth of the ongoing Communion of the saints in Heaven.

Remembering . . . So We'll Never Forget

Foretaste. That's what Moses' band of refugees would come to believe about their Passover experience. On that night God saved them. Because of that night they had a future. To this day, believing Jews celebrate the Feast of Unleavened Bread so they will never forget how God delivered them in the past. Neither do they want to forget their future, which is also in God's hands. So they celebrate.

With equal fervor, Christians remember how God delivered them from sin when Jesus died on the cross. They also remember the promises of a future Communion (community) among the saints. Forever.

We will not forget.

10
Out of Egypt!

Exodus 13:17–14:31; Matthew 2:13-23; Acts 2:36

You may have heard of the ten-year-old who, when asked what he had learned that morning in Sunday school, gave this full report to his mother. "Our teacher told us about when God sent Moses behind the enemy lines to rescue the Israelites from the Egyptians. When they came to the Red Sea, Moses called for the engineers to build a pontoon bridge. After they had all crossed, they looked back and saw the Egyptian tanks coming. Quick as a flash, Moses radioed headquarters on his walkie-talkie to send bombers to blow up the bridge and save the Israelites."

"Bobby," his surprised mother exclaimed, "is that really the way your teacher told the story?"

"Well, not exactly," he confessed. "But if I told it her way, you'd never believe it."

Bobby isn't the only person to have difficulty accepting the biblical version of the exodus, is he? It was only a few months ago that I was reading in a weekly newsmagazine of the ongoing scholarly debates over the trustworthiness of the Bible's account of the age of the patriarchs (Abraham, Isaac, and Jacob), the kingdoms of David and Solomon, and, of course, the exodus. It sounds a lot like the arguments that were popular when I was in college and for generations before then. Knowing how scholars love to quibble, I am completely confident the issues won't be settled in my lifetime or yours. So in this final chapter, we'll continue doing what we've been doing throughout this book. We'll take the Bible at face value. We want to concentrate on what is most important. Remember, this is not as much a story about Joseph or Jacob or Moses as it is about God. What is central to the whole exodus event is God's rescue of His people.

If you focus on the people, you'll become pretty disillusioned. The people who complained in slavery now complain in freedom. You wonder about them, don't you? Did they think their troubles would all be over if they could just get away from Pharaoh's grasp? How could they keep on doubting their God and His servant Moses? They had seen all the miracles, hadn't they? Yet after such tremendous displays of God's power, the moment they see Pharaoh's army approaching, they panic.

> They said to Moses, "Was it because there were no graves in Egypt that you brought us to the desert to die? What have you done to us by bringing us out of Egypt? Didn't we say to you in Egypt, 'Leave us alone; let us serve the Egyptians'? It would have been better for us to serve the Egyptians than to die in the desert!" (Exodus 14:11, 12)

We will hear more from the people later, but right now we will look at this event from Pharaoh's point of view.

The Exodus: Pharaoh's Point of View

"What have we done?" Like men rousing from a stupor, Pharaoh and his chief advisers wake up to the enormous economic hit their nation has just taken. In their own moment of panic, horrified at the carnage left by the angel of death and promising anything, anything to stop the bloodletting, the king had shouted Moses and his people out of the country. Now, still shaken but calmer, Pharaoh was hit by the truth. "We have let the Israelites go and have lost their services!" So Pharaoh calls for his chariots and marshals his army and charges after the Israelites. Not just any chariots. "The best chariots in Egypt." And not just several. "Several hundreds of them." And their officers "and more horsemen and troops" hurry to the chase. The king will be avenged. His economy must be saved.

The answer may seem obvious, but the question still needs to be posed. We know what Pharaoh did, but do we know why? I have already suggested the economic explanation: Egypt rested on a slave economy. You don't remove six hundred thousand workers from the labor force in a small country like Egypt without severe consequences. Who would do the dirty jobs? Where would the unskilled labor force come from? What about the gross domestic product and the economic stimulation provided by the Hebrew consumers?

His "Just Because" Reason

But it wasn't just the economy, not according to the Bible, anyway. We've become familiar with Pharaoh's hardened heart by now. One scriptural lesson is inescapable, as we saw earlier: God grants us the desires of our hearts. Here again is Psalm 37:4: "Delight yourself in the LORD and he will give you the desires of your heart." It can't be clearer than that.

The king wanted the Hebrews back in his Egyptian camp because . . . because . . . because the king wanted the Hebrews back in his Egyptian camp! It's about the economy, yes. But it's also about power, about dominion, about being god of your own universe. This is not merely a story about the national financial system, nor even a story about masters and slaves. It is a lesson, told before this and told hundreds of times after this, about God's way versus any other god's way. It's a tale of what happens when you defy, even in the name of God, whatever god commands the throne where you are. The current term for this phenomenon is spiritual warfare.

The apostle Paul, challenging Christians to be bold in the midst of spiritual battles, describes it this way: "For our struggle is not against flesh and blood, but against the rulers, against the authorities, against the powers of this dark world, and against the spiritual forces of evil in the heavenly realms" (Ephesians 6:12). The battle is spiritual; unfortunately, the warriors are people—individual persons confronting evil in their efforts to do right while being pulled toward the wrong; groups debating whether their core values will be righteous or opportunistic; nations rising up to defend themselves against tyrants and destroyers of human freedom and dignity.

Pharaoh wanted the Israelites back under his control *because*. Just because. It's only a step from his refusal to let the Israelites be themselves and Hitler's demented determination not to let the Jews be. Period. Just because they're Jews. No other explanation needed.

Study the globe today. Note the countries in which Christians are dying for their faith—not because they are a threat to the stability of the government, or because they are mistreating the non-Christians among whom they live, or because they are an armed menace or are militantly evangelistic. No. Just because they *are*.

It is often pointed out that more Christians died because of their faith in the twentieth century than in the previous nineteen. This fact often comes as a shock to naïve believers. They somehow feel that everything will be OK if they just follow Jesus. The awful truth, however, is that some of our troubles are ours *because* we follow Jesus, just as the Israelites' real source of trouble was that they were Israelites. Different. God-fearing. Government-defying.

When America was shaken to its foundation on September 11, 2001, terrorists had wrested control of four commercial planes and flown them to fiery destruction, causing the worst one-day toll of casualties in the history of the United States. Why? Why did they do it? Why did they hate Americans? Many explanations were offered. At bottom, though, they hated us because we *are*. They cite history to justify their actions, but their rationalizations don't convince. The truth is, they despise what we are and who we are. They despise us because we are not like them. They oppose us because our ancestors abused them. They hate us because we do not serve their god. And their god can't stand it.

The confrontation now, like the conflict between the ancient Egyptians and Israelites, is a battle of hearts. Toward the people of God, Pharaoh's hard heart beats cold; he would kill before he would be disobeyed.

God's heart beats warmly for His suffering people. In the Battle of the Monarchs, the earthly king's heart grew harder until he would stop at nothing to have his way. Motivated by a softened heart, the divine monarch did what was required to save His people. Ultimately, the gospel later reports, that loving heart would use a cross to save His people.

The Exodus: The Israelites' Point of View

Their reaction was so very human. When trouble hits, blame somebody. Anybody.

"It's your fault, Moses."

"What have *you* done to us, Moses?"

"It was better in Egypt, Moses."

They could stand anything, these griping refugees, but discomfort. Soon after their escape, the whining and the faultfinding began. If you're going to complain, you have to have somebody to blame. If things are bad, somebody must be at fault. That somebody, as it has been from the beginning of history until now, must be the leader.

They weren't only uncomfortable, these Hebrews. They were scared. So many of them, so few of us. Such fine armor, such magnificent horses, such disciplined soldiers. So much stronger than our side.

The Israelites were "terrified." Read their plaints again.

> They said to Moses, "Was it because there were no
> graves in Egypt that you brought us to the desert to die?
> What have you done to us by bringing us out of Egypt?
> Didn't we say to you in Egypt, 'Leave us alone; let us serve
> the Egyptians'? It would have been better for us to serve
> the Egyptians than to die in the desert" (Exodus 14:11, 12).

They were not only losing their nerve, but they were losing
their memories as well. "We didn't want to break away from
Egypt in the first place. You did this to us, Moses. We were per-
fectly content serving Pharaoh. And now we're going to die.
You, you, Moses, why couldn't you have left well enough
alone?"

Things just weren't turning out the way they expected. All
they wanted was to be happy. And happy they weren't.

Their "Right" to Be Happy

The story has a modern ring to it, doesn't it? It's the
American story long before there was an America to have a
story. For most of us, the American Dream is the right to be
happy. Isn't that what Thomas Jefferson wrote into the
Declaration of Independence—something about the rights of
life, liberty, and *the pursuit of happiness*? As fine a document as
the Declaration is, I prefer the Bible. It's more realistic. The
Bible promises blessing, joy, peace, companionship with God,
an eternal home with Him, and much, much more, but it does
not promise happiness in this life.

You can't help contrasting the Declaration's happiness and
Jefferson's own life, which was dogged by tragedy. At the age of
fourteen he lost his father. His sister, Elizabeth, was mentally
handicapped. He lost another sister when she was twenty-five
and his best friend and brother-in-law in his twenties. He and
his wife Martha had six children, but four of them died. Then
she herself died in childbirth in the tenth year of their marriage,
leaving him in a state of emotional collapse. His son-in-law

went mad and threatened his wife's life. Two of his nephews murdered and dismembered a slave for breaking a pitcher that had belonged to their mother. His granddaughter married an alcoholic who stabbed her brother.

As an old man, Jefferson confessed, "I have known what it is to lose every species of connection which is dear to the human heart: friends, brethren, parents, children. . . ." He had the right to pursue happiness, he thought, but it eluded him. Even now in the twenty-first century, it eludes his reputation.[39] There seems to be growing evidence that the hundreds of African-Americans who claim him as their ancestor have a case. He apparently sired several children by his African-American slave Sally Hemmings. He was in life and remains in death a controversial, enigmatic, troubled man. Yet he remains the hero of confused Americans who stoutly claim their "right" to happiness.

That's something Moses never promised.

You could correct me at this juncture if you wanted, citing Exodus 14:31: "And when the Israelites saw the great power the LORD displayed against the Egyptians, the people feared the LORD and put their trust in him and in Moses his servant." So they did. But if you have read ahead, you know that whenever the people became disgruntled again—as they did with maddening regularity—they yanked their trust from Moses and recalled once again the happiness they never knew in Egypt. Didn't they have every right, as Americans think we do, to happiness?

Aldous Huxley may have written the best commentary on the Israelites' (and Americans') preoccupation with comfort and happiness. The English author published *Brave New World* in 1932, but you would think it was a report on the current state of American nerves. In the "brave new world," happiness is not only pursued but caught—pain has been eliminated, struggle and discomfort are no more—thanks to *soma*, a wonder drug that calms your temper, makes you friends with your enemies, and transforms you into a patient, longsuffering soul without rancor or stress. "Christianity without tears," is how Huxley defined this new encapsulated virtue.

Near the close of the novel, though, a new character is introduced, a semisavage from the fringes of that anesthetized society. He gets to meet the controller of the world. He's not impressed. He doesn't want a tearless, stressless life. "It's too easy," he protests. "I don't want comfort. I want God. I want poetry. I want real danger. I want freedom. I want goodness…" When the controller insists that any other kind of civilization besides his brave new world would cause the savage to be unhappy, he answers, "I claim the right to be unhappy."[40]

That may be, in fact, one of our greatest freedoms. That may be why Jesus would not promise us Christianity without tears. His disciples would know what love means and that goodness involves struggle and pain and mourning. The Israelites were safe in Egypt, no doubt. They were also slaves.

And apparently, even beyond the borders of Egypt, they kept their slave mentality. It's not easily given up, this slavishness, particularly when people prefer comfort to freedom.

The Exodus: Moses' Point of View

"Don't be afraid."

"Stand firm."

"The Lord will fight for you."

"You will see the deliverance the Lord will bring you today."

Where did his confidence come from? With all the people moaning and crying, with the mood turning sour, how did he maintain any semblance of serenity? The Lord had done great things through him, granted, but such victories often give way to depths of despondency. Ask almost any preacher how he feels on Monday, after he has given his best on Sunday. Ask almost any performer how she feels once the show is over, when the lights are out and the crowds have gone home and she's alone to review her mistakes. Depression is the dogged pursuer of high achievers. Especially when, although you have given your best, the crowd turns against you.

Frederick Holliday would explain this to you if he could, but it's too late. Citizens of Cleveland, Ohio, were shaken in the mid-eighties when their high-achieving school superintendent was found crumpled in a stairwell at the city's Aviation High School, shot through the heart with a .357 magnum. This man was no loser. Holliday's list of accomplishments was one to be envied: first African-American superintendent the city had ever had; $36 million school levy approved by the voters; raises for the teachers; successful start of an aggressive building renovation program. He was an impressive man with an impressive record, but he killed himself.

His suicide note left no doubt where the fault lay: "I have had great success as a schoolman and a leader. I have enjoyed until now being your superintendent. As of this moment, it appears that my last piece of dignity is being stripped. The fighting among school board members and what petty politics is doing to the system has sickened me."

One more leader brought down by the people he was leading.

His Strength in the Lord

What kept Moses going? Why didn't his people's carping bring him down? He wasn't immune. If you've read the rest of Moses' story, you know of his bouts of near despair, of how tempted he was to quit, how earnestly he would plead his case and his people's before the Lord.

Before the Lord. There's the secret we're looking for. His strength was in the Lord, not in the approval of the masses.

It helps sometimes to read the biographies of achievers to learn the secrets of their endurance. It doesn't matter the field we study. We find the same need to ignore the carping of the crowd and draw our strength from on high. Consider a certain famous musician, for example. Handel's *Messiah*, one of the most popular compositions ever written, has inspired centuries of music lovers and God lovers. Everybody knows how he whipped off the inspired music in twenty-four days without once leaving his house. To this day, orchestras and choirs all

over the Western world stage special productions of this
eighteenth-century masterpiece. Handel's music takes them to
the gates of Heaven.

What everybody doesn't know is how his critics dogged
him. Romain Rolland describes his torment graphically. "He
was surrounded by a crowd of bulldogs with terrible fangs, by
unmusical men of letters who were likewise able to bite, by
jealous colleagues, arrogant virtuosos, cannibalistic theatrical
companies, fashionable cliques, feminine plots, and nationalis-
tic leagues. . . . Twice he was bankrupt, and once he was strick-
en by apoplexy amid the ruins of his company. But he always
found his feet again; he never gave in."[41]

He never gave in, it must be added, because he had learned
not to look to an adoring audience for his strength. There is a
reason we speak of the fickle crowd!

He had learned what the apostle Paul found out centuries
earlier. In 2 Corinthians 11:21-29, an exasperated Paul defends
himself against his critics. He reminds his readers of his Jewish
credentials as a descendant of Abraham and his more important credentials as a servant of Christ. Then he catalogs the
abuse he has suffered for the Lord—the hard labor, imprisonments, floggings, stonings, and shipwrecks:

> I have been in danger from rivers, in danger from ban-
> dits, in danger from my own countrymen, in danger from
> Gentiles; in danger in the city, in danger in the country, in
> danger at sea; and in danger from false brothers. I have
> labored and toiled and have often gone without sleep; I
> have known hunger and thirst and have often gone with-
> out food; I have been cold and naked. Besides everything
> else, I face daily the pressure of my concern for all the
> churches (2 Corinthians 11:26, 27).

In the midst of all the tribulations, he faced "danger from
false brothers." The fickle crowd.

It is no wonder that to other friends, Paul wrote, "Rejoice in
the Lord always; I will say it again: Rejoice!" (In the Lord, not

in the crowd.) How could he write so positively, he who had suffered so much for his faith? Here is his answer: "I have learned to be content whatever the circumstances . . . whether well fed or hungry, whether living in plenty or in want. I can do everything through him who gives me strength" (Philippians 4:4, 11-13).

Thus Moses, laboring under circumstances so adverse we can barely imagine them, had to find his strength in the Lord. There was no one else, not even his siblings Aaron and Miriam, whose judgment he could always trust, whose steadiness under fire would not waver. His closest confidant was his lieutenant Joshua, and at times even he could not share Moses' burden. His trust had to be in the Lord. In Him was his strength.

Another Flight to Egypt

We have come to the end of our study. God has liberated His people. Egypt will never again play such an important role in the history of Israel. However, in the history of the world, Egypt will once again come to center stage, but not for any greatness of its own. There will be another flight to Egypt, retracing the route of Jacob and his relatives. Jacob fled with his family and flocks in search of food. In this later flight, undertaken by another Joseph and wife and baby, not food but safety will be the concern. As the power-crazed Pharaoh pursued the fleeing Israelites, a maddened, baby-killing King Herod will unwittingly drive this little family to Egypt to preserve the life of their baby.

To Matthew, there is much more to his story than just getting the family out of town and into safety. He sees the hand of God at work once more. He tells us that Joseph, Mary, and Jesus stayed in Egypt until Herod was dead and it was safe to return to Nazareth, Joseph's hometown. What appears to be a simple return of refugees from the land of safety is far more. As

Matthew explains, "And so was fulfilled what the Lord had said through the prophet: 'Out of Egypt I called my son'" (2:15). That Son, Peter would announce on the Day of Pentecost, "God has made . . . both Lord and Christ" (Acts 2:36).

We started this study tracing the fortunes of the family of Jacob. Our journey has introduced such topics as sibling rivalry, wise and foolish parenting, leadership qualities and strategies, power struggles in high places and low, divine miracles and human manipulation, and memory and the meaning of community. The story pitted the powerless descendants of Jacob against the might of nearly all-powerful monarchs. It has been Egypt versus Israel, Pharaoh versus Moses, and finally, Herod versus a baby. If you and I had been there, our money would have been on the monarchs. Slaves, unarmed generals, and little babies simply do not overturn thrones.

Unless God says so.

And in this case, God said so.

Endnotes

[1] John W. Gardner, *On Leadership* (New York: Simon and Schuster, Inc., 1990), p. xi.

[2] Steven F. Hayward, *Churchill on Leadership* (Rocklin, CA: Prima Publishing, 1997), p. 6.

[3] Gardner, p. 23.

[4] Colin L. Powell, *My American Journey* (New York: Random House, 1995), p. 264.

[5] Peter Hay, *Canned Laughter* (New York: Ticknor and Fields, 1992), p. 97.

[6] Thomas Mallon, *A Book of One's Own* (New York: Ticknor and Fields, 1984), p. xvi.

[7] Quoted by Charles W. Colson, "Standing Tough Against All Odds," *Christianity Today*, September 6, 1985, p. 29.

[8] Merv Budd, "No Statute of Limitations for Forgiveness," *Leadership Magazine*, Spring 1998, p. 77.

[9] R.C. Lewontin, *New York Review of Books*. Quoted in *Context*, June 1996, p. 5.

[10] J.M. Cohen, ed., *The Rider Book of Mystical Verse* (London: Rider and Company, 1983), p. 125.

[11] Carl Sandburg, *Abraham Lincoln: The War Years*, Volume 3 (New York: Harcourt, Brace and Co., 1939), p. 225.

[12] "Tribe Is Thicker Than Water," *Context*, November 15, 1998. Citation taken from *New York Review of Books*, June 11, 1998.

[13] Joshua Halberstam, *Everyday Ethics* (New York: Viking, the Penguin Group, 1993), p. 161.

[14] Marian Wright Edelman, *The Measure of Our Success* (Boston: Beacon Press, 1992), p. 11.

[15] "Intellectuals as Racists," *Time*, March 13, 1964, p. 102.

[16] Robert J. Ringer, *Looking Out for #1* (New York: Random House, 1978), p. 106.

[17] Robert E. Luccock, *Halford Luccock Treasury*, p. 395.

[18] Hans Kung, *On Being a Christian* (New York: Doubleday and Company, 1976), p. 168.

[19] Gwen Bagni and Paul Dubov, *Backstairs at the White House* (Englewood Cliffs, NJ: Prentice-Hall, 1978), p. 65.

[20] Carl Sandburg, *Abraham Lincoln: The Prairie Years* (New York: Harcourt, Brace, 1926), p. 223.

[21] J.F.O. McAllister, "Atrocity and Outrage," *Time*, August 17, 1992, p. 21.

[22] Ibid, p. 28.

[23] "The Reciprocal Missionary," *Reader's Digest*, September 1963, p. 10.

[24] Hugh Sidey, "Never Yearning for Home," *Time*, February, 13, 1984, p. 16.

[25] Omar Bradley, *Bradley: A Soldier's Story* (Chicago: Rand McNally and Co., 1951), p. 52.

[26] Richard M. Nixon, *Leaders* (New York: Warner Books, 1982), p. 13.

[27] Thomas J. Peters and Robert H. Waterman, Jr., *In Search of Excellence* (New York: Harper and Row, 1982), p. 225.

[28] Richard M. Nixon, *Leaders*, p. 23.

[29] Henry Troyat, *Tolstoy* (New York: Doubleday and Co., 1967), p. 444.

[30] E. Stanley Jones, *Christ and Human Suffering* (Nashville, TN: Abingdon Press, 1933), p. 112.

[31] Nikos Kazantzakis, *St. Francis* (New York: Simon and Schuster, 1962), p. 90.

[32] Sheldon B. Kopp, *If You Meet the Buddha on the Road, Kill Him!* (Palo Alto, CA: Science and Behavior Books, Inc., 1972), p. 106.

[33] "Not Getting Involved," *Time*, May 15, 1964, p. 72.

[34] Nikita Khrushchev, *Khrushchev Remembers* (Boston: Little, Brown, and Company, 1974), p. 187.

[35] Harry Golden, *The Right Time* (New York: Pyramid Books, 1969), p. 30.

[36] James A. Pike, *A Time for Christian Candor* (New York: Harper and Row, 1964), p. 63.

[37] Harold Kushner, *To Life!* (Boston: Little, Brown, and Company, 1993), p. 10.

[38] Larry Lutz, "A Tender Communion, Somewhere in China," *Christianity Today*, December 11, 1981, p. 42.

[39] Page Smith, *The Shaping of America*, Volume 3 (New York: McGraw-Hill, 1980), p. 576.

[40] Aldous Huxley, *Brave New World* (London: Chatto and Windos, 1932), p. 240.

[41] Romaine Rolland, "Handel: Desire to Make Them Better," *Eternity*, March 1980, p. 44.